"'R.C. Sproul,' someone said to me in the 1970s, 'is the finest communicator in the Reformed world.' Now, four decades later, his skills honed by long practice, his understanding deepened by years of prayer, meditation, and testing (as Martin Luther counseled), R.C. shares the fruit of what became perhaps his greatest love: feeding and nourishing his own congregation at St. Andrew's from the Word of God and building them up in faith and fellowship and in Christian living and serving. Dr. Sproul's expositional commentaries have all R.C.'s hallmarks: clarity and liveliness, humor and pathos, always expressed in application to the mind, will, and affections. R.C.'s ability to focus on 'the big picture,' his genius of never saying too much, leaving his hearers satisfied yet wanting more, never making the Word dull, are all present in these expositions. They are his gift to the wider church. May they nourish God's people well and serve as models of the kind of ministry for which we continue to hunger."

—Dr. Sinclair B. Ferguson
Teaching Fellow
Ligonier Ministries

"Dr. R.C. Sproul, well known as a master theologian and extraordinary communicator, showed that he was a powerful, insightful, helpful expository preacher. This collection of sermons is of great value for churches and Christians everywhere."

—Dr. W. Robert Godfrey
President emeritus and professor of church history emeritus
Westminster Seminary California, Escondido, California

"I tell my students again and again, 'You need to buy good commentaries and do so with some discernment.' Among them there must be preacher's commentaries, for not all commentaries are the same. Some may tell you what the text means but provide little help in answering the question, 'How do I preach this text?' Dr. R.C. Sproul was a legend in our time. His preaching held us in awe for half a century, and these pages represent the fruit of his exposition at the very peak of his abilities and insights. Dr. Sproul's expositional commentary series represents Reformed theology on fire, delivered from a pastor's heart in a vibrant congregation. Essential reading."

—Dr. Derek W.H. Thomas
Senior minister
First Presbyterian Church, Columbia, South Carolina

"Dr. R.C. Sproul was the premier theologian of our day, an extraordinary instrument in the hand of the Lord. Possessed with penetrating insight into the text of Scripture, Dr. Sproul was a gifted expositor and world-class teacher, endowed with a strategic grasp and command of the inspired Word. When he stepped into the pulpit of St. Andrew's and committed himself to the weekly discipline of biblical exposition, this noted preacher demonstrated a rare ability to explicate and apply God's Word. I wholeheartedly recommend Dr. Sproul's expositional commentaries to all who long to know the truth better and experience it more deeply in a life-changing fashion. Here is an indispensable tool for digging deeper into God's Word. This is a must-read for every Christian."

—Dr. Steven J. Lawson
Founder and president
OnePassion Ministries, Dallas

"How exciting! Thousands of us have long been indebted to Dr. R.C. Sproul the teacher, and now, through Dr. Sproul's expositional commentaries, we are indebted to Sproul the preacher, whose sermons are thoroughly biblical, soundly doctrinal, warmly practical, and wonderfully readable. Sproul masterfully presents us with the 'big picture' of each pericope in a dignified yet conversational style that accentuates the glory of God and meets the real needs of sinful people like us. This series of volumes is an absolute must for every Reformed preacher and church member who yearns to grow in the grace and knowledge of Christ Jesus. I predict that Sproul's pulpit ministry in written form will do for Christians in the twenty-first century what Martyn Lloyd-Jones' sermonic commentaries did for us last century. *Tolle lege*, and buy these volumes for your friends."

—Dr. Joel R. Beeke
President and professor of systematic theology and homiletics
Puritan Reformed Theological Seminary, Grand Rapids, Michigan

GALATIANS

AN EXPOSITIONAL COMMENTARY

GALATIANS

AN EXPOSITIONAL COMMENTARY

R.C. SPROUL

LIGONIER MINISTRIES

Galatians: An Expositional Commentary
© 2022 by the R.C. Sproul Trust

Published by Ligonier Ministries
421 Ligonier Court, Sanford, FL 32771
Ligonier.org

Printed in China
RR Donnelley
0000422
First edition

ISBN 978-1-64289-424-0 (Hardcover)
ISBN 978-1-64289-425-7 (ePub)
ISBN 978-1-64289-426-4 (Kindle)

Cover design: Ligonier Creative
Interior typeset: Katherine Lloyd, The DESK

Library of Congress Control Number: 9781642894240

CONTENTS

SERIES PREFACE

When God called me into full-time Christian ministry, He called me to the academy. I was trained and ordained to a ministry of teaching, and most of my adult life has been devoted to preparing young men for the Christian ministry and to trying to bridge the gap between seminary and Sunday school through various means under the aegis of Ligonier Ministries.

Then, in 1997, God did something I never anticipated: He placed me in the position of preaching weekly as a leader of a congregation of His people—St. Andrew's in Sanford, Florida. Over the past twelve years, as I have opened the Word of God on a weekly basis for these dear saints, I have come to love the task of the local minister. Though my role as a teacher continues, I am eternally grateful to God that He saw fit to place me in this new ministry, the ministry of a preacher.

Very early in my tenure with St. Andrew's, I determined that I should adopt the ancient Christian practice of *lectio continua*, "continuous expositions," in my preaching. This method of preaching verse-by-verse through books of the Bible (rather than choosing a new topic each week) has been attested throughout church history as the one approach that ensures believers hear the full counsel of God. Therefore, I began preaching lengthy series of messages at St. Andrew's, eventually working my way through several biblical books in a practice that continues to the present day.

Previously, I had taught through books of the Bible in various settings, including Sunday school classes, Bible studies, and audio and video teaching series for Ligonier Ministries. But now I found myself appealing not so much to the minds of my hearers but to both their minds and their hearts.

I knew that I was responsible as a preacher to clearly explain God's Word *and* to show how we ought to live in light of it. I sought to fulfill both tasks as I ascended the St. Andrew's pulpit each week.

What you hold in your hand, then, is a written record of my preaching labors amidst my beloved Sanford congregation. The dear saints who sit under my preaching encouraged me to give my sermons a broader hearing. To that end, the chapters that follow were adapted from a sermon series I preached at St. Andrew's.

Please be aware that this book is part of a broader series of books containing adaptations of my St. Andrew's sermons. This book, like all the others in the series, will *not* give you the fullest possible insight into each and every verse in this biblical book. Though I sought to at least touch on each verse, I focused on the key themes and ideas that comprised the "big picture" of each passage I covered. Therefore, I urge you to use this book as an overview and introduction.

I pray that you will be as blessed in reading this material as I was in preaching it.

—R.C. Sproul
Lake Mary, Florida
April 2009

1

APOSTOLIC GREETING

Galatians 1:1–5

Paul, an apostle—not from men nor through man, but through Jesus Christ and God the Father, who raised him from the dead—and all the brothers who are with me,

To the churches of Galatia:

Grace to you and peace from God our Father and the Lord Jesus Christ, who gave himself for our sins to deliver us from the present evil age, according to the will of our God and Father, to whom be the glory forever and ever. Amen.

There are several questions, as there always are, that tend to matters of authorship, date, and destination of books in the Bible. Paul's letter to the Galatians is no exception. We don't know the exact order in which Paul's letters were written, but the majority report is that in all probability, this letter from the Apostle Paul was the first.

The audience is also a question. It is addressed **to the churches of Galatia** (v. 2), but that is a region, not a city. The region of Galatia was in central Asia Minor, in what is now Turkey. We don't know whether the destination was the northern territory of Galatia, the southern province of Galatia, or possibly both, as it was a circular letter addressed to more than one church. We don't know for certain when Paul wrote the letter, but it could have been written as early as AD 48, just a few years after the ascension of our Lord into heaven.

We know, in any case, that regardless of which churches were intended to receive the letter, they were having problems. Of all the epistles Paul wrote, this one is clearly the most fiery. In this respect, it is a unique letter. Paul, who we know had such a tender pastor's heart, wrote this epistle in a spirit of righteous indignation. As we begin to explore this letter, we will discover why he was so indignant.

It begins quite simply with an identification of the name of **Paul** (v. 1). I remember when my mentor, Dr. John Gerstner, spoke of the Apostle Paul. To describe his personality and his character, he used Paul's name as an acrostic, saying *P* stood for "polluted" because Paul understood that he was the chief of sinners, and the *A* referred to his "office" as an Apostle. But of most striking significance to me was that Dr. Gerstner said the *U* in Paul's name stood for "uncompromising" and the *L* stood for "loving." Dr. Gerstner explained that we normally think the quality of being uncompromising is not a virtue but a vice, a reflection of somebody who is rigid and stiff, unbending and relentless in his views. This is the exact contrast of what we expect from somebody who is loving. Then he went on to say that Paul was not only uncompromising, but he was loving. Dr. Gerstner wouldn't allow this to be understood in unethical terms; rather, he said Paul was uncompromising and *therefore* loving. The reason Paul refused to be compromising, as we clearly see in this letter to the Galatians, is that he was never ever willing to negotiate the gospel of Jesus Christ.

Paul would be patient, tender, and long-suffering about a host of debates and issues raised in the various churches that he founded and to whom he ministered, but when it came to the gospel, there was no wiggle room in Paul because he loved the gospel. More importantly, he loved the Lord of the gospel. His heart was filled to overflowing with affection for Jesus. Not only did he love the gospel of Jesus and love Jesus Himself, but he loved his congregations. He loved those people to whom he ministered. He had such a depth of affection and concern for them that he would never think of compromising the gospel to be popular with them or to be politically correct in their eyes. He loved them far too much for that.

He further identifies himself at the beginning of this epistle, as he often does on other occasions, as **an apostle** (v. 1). We've heard that term *Apostle* again and again, and in common jargon, we tend to see two words as synonyms: disciple and Apostle. However, they're not synonyms. They don't refer to the same thing, even though they represent the same people on certain occasions. The term *disciple* means a "learner" or a "student." The term Apostle means something far more than that in its literal meaning.

The Greek word *apostolos* means "someone who has been sent," but what is meant is not just an everyday messenger for an everyday task. When my mother sent me to the grocery store to buy a loaf of bread, she did not thereby ordain me as an Apostle. Rather, Apostles were sent from a particular authoritative person and carried that person's particular authority. Jesus had many disciples, more than seventy, and He chose from among that group of disciples only twelve to whom He would confer the authority and the office of Apostleship. Who, though, is the greatest Apostle we meet in the New Testament? You may say Peter, or you may be inclined to say Paul. Wasn't Paul of singular importance as the Apostle to the gentiles?

Neither Peter nor Paul deserves the rank of chief Apostle in the New Testament. The supreme Apostle in the New Testament is Jesus Himself, who from all eternity was ordained by the Father and sent into the world by the Father's authority to fulfill a mission. The eternal second person of the Trinity took upon Himself a human nature to fulfill the task that the Father had given Him, and He was empowered by the Holy Spirit to carry out that mission from the Father. As Jesus said, "I do not speak on my own authority" (John 14:10), and "All authority in heaven and on earth has been given to me" (Matt. 28:18).

An apostle in the ancient world was an emissary who had been confirmed by an authority or a ruler such as a king and who was authorized to speak in the name of that authority. By speaking in the name of that person, he carried with him the supreme authority of the one who sent him. Jesus was the supreme Apostle. The authority that the Father gave Him was then transferred by Him to a small group of men who spoke with the authority of Christ, who in turn spoke with the authority of God.

If you don't like what Paul says or what Peter says, you're rejecting the authority of Jesus. If you reject the authority of Jesus, you reject the authority of God the Father. When Paul identifies himself with his official title **Paul, an apostle**, he is claiming divine authority, and such authority can impose duties and obligations on anyone who hears his voice. Paul wastes no time in using this authority to respond to a very significant issue in the Galatian region.

A heresy had developed among the Galatians, and it threatened and denied the very gospel. It threatened the authority of Christ. This pernicious heresy is known as the Judaizing heresy, and it argued that to be a Christian, you must continue to practice the rituals and the ceremonies of the Old Testament law. This would, by implication, deny the sufficiency of the sacrifice of Christ. The group that promulgated this heresy, known as the Judaizers, denied that the Jewish ceremonial rules and rituals were perfectly and absolutely fulfilled by the finished work of Jesus Christ. For them to insist on the continuity of those former things was, by implication, to empty their fulfillment by Jesus Christ.

Those who were in effect denying the gospel and denying the Christ of the gospel were quick to argue that Paul, who had founded the churches in the region of Galatia, did not have the authority of an Apostle. In arguing against the gospel, they were also arguing against the credentials of Paul. At the very beginning of this epistle, with his writing instrument ready to explode in his hands, Paul says: "Now hear this: This is the Apostle Paul speaking. I'm not simply an itinerant missionary or the founder of the church among the Galatians, but I am an Apostle."

In the early church, a controversial question concerned the authenticity of the Apostleship of Paul. There were criteria set forth in the book of Acts to select a replacement among the Apostles. To be an Apostle, one first had to have been a disciple of Jesus Christ during His earthly ministry. Second, one had to have been an eyewitness of the resurrection. Third, one had to have been called directly and immediately by Jesus to fill that role.

We look at the book of Acts and see that the Apostle Paul was not a disciple during the earthly ministry of Jesus. Paul says that he did not know Jesus according to the flesh and that he was not an eyewitness of the resurrection, at least not before the ascension. Indeed, Paul says that Christ appeared to him as "one untimely born" (1 Cor. 15:8) on the road to Damascus. The most critical and significant criterion to be an Apostle was to have a direct and immediate call from Jesus.

Some argue that one of the main reasons that Luke wrote the book of Acts was not only to give a history of the early church and the expansion from Jerusalem to the ends of the earth but also to defend the authenticity of Paul's Apostolic authority. Three times in the book of Acts, Luke recounts the circumstances of Paul's call by Christ to be an Apostle (chs. 9; 22; 26).

As we learn in Acts, Paul—then called Saul—was told after being commissioned by Jesus to be an Apostle that he was to return to Jerusalem to meet with some of the other elder statesmen among the young church so that his Apostolic authority could be confirmed (Acts 9:6, 10–19). The Apostle Paul, according to the first-century Christian community, was public enemy number one. He was the man who had been breathing out fire, who went from city to city dragging Christians from their homes, and who subjected them to severe persecution even unto death (Acts 8:1–3; 9:1–2). Here's the man who stood on the sidelines holding the clothes of those who were throwing stones to kill Stephen (Acts 7:58).

Paul's reputation was well known in Jerusalem; he was a Christian killer who hated the church and wanted to destroy it. After his conversion, he came to the church claiming to be an Apostle. There was great suspicion and great reluctance in the early Christian community to accept the authentic reality of Paul's being an Apostle.

It is no small matter to claim Apostleship. The Old Testament prophets and the New Testament Apostles spoke with God's authority. Prophets and Apostles were holders of offices established by God and agents through which God would speak. When Jeremiah made his announcements to the Old Testament people of Israel, he didn't say, "In my humble opinion." He prefaced his remarks by saying, "Thus says the Lord." A prophet with a capital *P* was entitled to make that announcement only because he could verify that he had been called by God and given the authority to speak on God's behalf. Just as the Old Testament prophet was an agent of revelation commissioned by God, the New Testament Apostle was authorized by God Himself, not by appointment to office by men through the voting of a congregation or some such means.

Paul, an apostle—not from men nor through man (v. 1). It's as though Paul is saying: "I didn't get my call from Peter, James, and John or through Ananias or anyone else in the early Christian community. They may have received me and recognized me and confirmed me, but it wasn't as though they elected me to be an Apostle and then looked for Christ to confirm that call. The source of my authority is not from the other Apostles but rather from Jesus Christ and God the Father."

Jesus had said earlier to those whom He had commissioned with authority, "Whoever receives you receives me" (Matt. 10:40). In radical feminist theology, we've heard it said repeatedly that the Apostle Paul was a misogynist who was opposed to women; therefore, such radicals comment, "Jesus I love, but Paul is unacceptable to me." The problem is that if you reject Paul, you reject the One who sent him, Jesus; and if you reject the One who sent Jesus, you reject the Father, for Paul says he received his call **through Jesus Christ and God the Father, who raised him from the dead** (v. 1).

You can't have Jesus and not have Paul. You can't receive Jesus and reject Peter. These men were Apostles speaking by divine authority. Ephesians 2:19–21 and 3:1–5 state that the foundation of the church itself is the prophets and the Apostles. If you shake that foundation, questioning the authority of the Apostles, you weaken and destroy the foundation of the church. That's what's happening in our contemporary culture that wants to hold on to Jesus but get rid of Paul.

Paul writes on behalf of **all the brothers who are with me, To the churches of Galatia** (vv. 1–2). And then he gives his common greeting: **Grace to you and peace from God our Father and the Lord Jesus Christ** (v. 3). How many times have you read that in the New Testament? This is common in Paul's writing. What's uncommon in this epistle is that usually after he gives the personal greetings, he will then go on to say something like "I am so pleased to hear of your ministry that's going out to all the world, and I'm praying for you" (see Rom. 1:8–15; 1 Cor. 1:4–9; Phil. 1:3–11; Col. 1:3–14). There's none of that in the epistle to the Galatians because Paul is not pleased with the Galatians. He's doing battle with them. He's eminently displeased with the reports that he is getting about these churches that have entertained the Judaizing heresy. And yet he still uses the terms **Grace to you and peace**. Have you ever wondered about those terms that are used for greetings in the Scriptures?

Do you think the authors borrowed from literary traditions invented by their contemporary culture in the same way that we would write "Dear so-and-so" in letters today? No, this greeting was not mere convention. These words **grace** and **peace** were carefully chosen by God the Holy Spirit as a way of greeting those who were beloved in the Savior. The first of the two greetings is **grace**. Before Paul begins to expound the content of this epistle, he starts with the word **grace**, which is the very thing being undermined by the Judaizers in the Galatian churches. The Judaizers proclaimed a different way of salvation, a different gospel. They proclaimed a gospel that added works to grace. Paul reminds the Galatians of grace in his very greeting. He might have said *sola gratia*, grace alone, because that's part of the theme of this epistle.

The Hebrew term for **peace** was *shalom*. When the Jews met each other, they would exchange the greeting *shalom aleichem, aleichem shalom*: "Peace be to you and to you, peace." This peace is not simply the cessation of warfare with earthly enemies or even some nice inner feeling of contentment and tranquility. The ultimate desire for the Jew was to have peace with God, the end of antagonism, the end of war with the Creator. Paul labors the point in his letters that the reason we need the gospel and that we need reconciliation is that by nature we are at enmity with God. When we are justified by faith, we have peace with God and we have access to His presence (see Rom. 5:1–2).

Grace to you and peace from God our Father and the Lord Jesus Christ, who gave himself for our sins (vv. 3–4). From the beginning, Paul is reasserting and reaffirming the gospel that he had proclaimed to the Galatians when he founded the church, the gospel of a redeeming Savior **who gave himself for our sins to deliver us from the present evil age, according to the will of our God and Father** (v. 4). The greeting is made complete with his benediction, his doxology, **to whom be the glory forever and ever. Amen** (v. 5).

Looking at the Greek, we see there is a repetition here. **To whom be the glory.** Presently or for a short time or for the next five years? No. Paul is not even satisfied by saying God is the One to whom the glory should be given forever. Rather, to make sure we don't miss the point, Paul exclaims, **to whom be the glory forever and ever**. At no time will the glory of God cease, even if the Galatians allow heretics among them who undermine God's gospel and Paul's authority.

2

ANOTHER GOSPEL

Galatians 1:6–9

I am astonished that you are so quickly deserting him who called you in the grace of Christ and are turning to a different gospel—not that there is another one, but there are some who trouble you and want to distort the gospel of Christ. But even if we or an angel from heaven should preach to you a gospel contrary to the one we preached to you, let him be accursed. As we have said before, so now I say again: If anyone is preaching to you a gospel contrary to the one you received, let him be accursed.

Rudolf Bultmann was one of the most controversial New Testament scholars of the twentieth century. He wrote many books, including *Kerygma and Myth*, in which he argued that the New Testament documents were replete with cleverly designed mythology. According to Bultmann, for a person to receive any benefit from reading the New Testament and the possible elements of historical reality contained within the Bible, he first had to follow Bultmann's program of demythologizing sacred Scripture. While I was studying Bultmann in graduate school, my professor, Professor G.C. Berkouwer, said of Bultmann, "Theology can sink no lower." Dr. Berkouwer hadn't yet seen the work of the post-Bultmannians who took demythologization to an even lower degree.

One of the things that Bultmann did was follow *form criticism*, a technique of analyzing the New Testament documents. Briefly, form criticism followed the assumption that the New Testament writings were the result of a lengthy tradition that was passed on orally and then finally codified in the written documents of the New Testament. As they sought to determine how the New Testament documents came to us, these scholars looked at certain patterns or structures or forms that perhaps could be detected in the documents of the New Testament. Bultmann was particularly interested in the miracle stories of the New Testament, which he rejected out of hand and consigned to the level of myth. He saw the repetition of a certain pattern or form in these New Testament miracle stories.

The pattern went something like this: When Jesus encountered someone in dire circumstances of misery or suffering or even death, He exercised His power as the incarnate Word of God and would miraculously heal the blind and the deaf and those who were crippled or dead. Then, that pattern was repeated by Jesus for others in need. Jesus performed a miraculous cure of a person's situation, and the climax was always the same. Those who observed these works of Jesus acknowledged their enormous surprise, amazement, or astonishment.

Bultmann analyzed that pattern and noted that every time Jesus healed someone, the onlookers were always astonished. How could you refute such an analysis? I think probably the most academic way you could refute the conclusions of Bultmann and his form criticism is by using one word: *duh*. What would you expect? If there was a real Jesus meeting people with real maladies who were cured by His real power, what do you think they would do? Be bored? Indifferent? Of course they were astonished.

There's a word in the Greek that occurs again and again in this pattern of miracle stories. The word is a form of the verb *thaumazō*, which is translated "to marvel" or "to be astonished." I note all that background for one word to point to what Paul says when he begins his response to the Galatians: *Thaumazō*. **I am astonished** (v. 6). When Paul uses that word *thaumazō*, he's not saying, "I'm a little bit concerned about this matter and a little surprised about what I'm hearing and the reports coming out of Galatia." No, he is registering Apostolic shock beyond measure.

One of the interesting views of this word comes from Martin Luther, whose favorite book of all his works was his commentary on Galatians. Luther, not known for his temperate language, read this statement by Paul and saw in it a soft aspect of Paul's rebuke. How Luther found any softness in Paul's statement here is beyond my comprehension. I don't think Paul was pulling any punches by using the term *thaumazō*. It's as though he exclaimed, "I cannot believe what you have done!"

I am astonished that you are so quickly deserting him who called you in the grace of Christ and are turning to a different gospel (v. 6). There are two things about which Paul was astonished. First, there was the substance of the issue: the Galatians were moving away from the gospel they had learned from him to a **different gospel**, to another gospel. Added to that astonishment was the second element: they moved away **so quickly**. It's as though Paul is saying: "What's wrong with you people? Not only have you moved away from the gospel, but I was hardly gone from your midst before you turned in another direction and began listening to the heretics who are distorting the gospel that you heard preached among you."

In 1546, in his very last sermon, Martin Luther, having returned to the place of his birth to settle a dispute among nobles, said something like this:

> In times past, we would have run to the ends of the world if we had known of a place where we could have heard God speak. But now that we hear the Word of God every day in sermons, indeed now that all books are full of it, we don't see it happening anymore. You hear at home in your house; father and mother and children sing and speak of the gospel. The preacher speaks of it in his parish church. You ought to lift up your hands and rejoice that we have been given the honor of hearing God speaking to us through His Word. Now people say, "What is that? After all, there's preaching every day, often many times every day so that we soon grow weary of it. What do we get out of it?" All, go ahead, dear brother. If you don't want God to speak to you every day in your house or in your church, then look for something to replace it. In Trier is our Lord God's coat and in Aachen are Joseph's pants and our Blessed Lady's chemise. Go there. Squander your money. Buy indulgences and the pope's secondhand junk.

Luther was saying, "Aren't we stupid and crazy when we've discovered the blessed gospel that came out of the darkness and into the light and we ignore or distort it?" How quickly, even near the end of Luther's life, people were returning to relics, putting their faith not in the gospel of Jesus Christ to be saved but in "Joseph's pants" and the "pope's secondhand junk." There were twenty-nine years between Luther's posting of the Ninety-Five Theses on the church door in Wittenberg and his last sermon. Perhaps it wasn't as short a time as it was for the Galatians to depart from the gospel as it took for the people of Germany to go back and to put their trust in indulgences and relics rather than in Christ.

We live in a time when there are few Protestants who have any understanding of what it is that Protestants are protesting and, frankly, very few Roman Catholics who have a clue about what Roman Catholicism teaches. I have said to my students who have been in the ministry for five years and are doing their doctoral work in my classroom, "You men of the gospel, you ministers, let me go to the blackboard and write down the elements of the gospel," and I ask, "What is the gospel?" They'll say, "God has a wonderful plan for your life," "God gives you a purpose-driven life," "God forgives your sins," or "God gives purpose and meaning to your existence."

It's rare when among ten ministers I can find more than one who can define the gospel. They don't know what it is. It may be true that Jesus forgives your sins, it may be true that you have purpose, and it may be true that you have meaning. All those things are wonderful, but that's not the gospel. The gospel is a distinct message with a distinct content that has to do with the person and work of Jesus Christ and how the benefits of His person and work are appropriated by faith and by faith alone.

Paul, in his amazement, says, "*Thaumazō*; I can't believe it, that you so quickly . . ." and then he uses the word "to desert." He grieves over how quickly the Galatians are **deserting him**. He's not saying, "I'm astonished that you are so quickly deserting *me*" but rather that they are deserting Him **who called you in the grace of Christ** (v. 6). That "Him" is God Himself. Paul says, "I can't believe how fast you have deserted God, how fast you've betrayed Christ, how fast you have left the gospel and are turning now to a different gospel."

This particular phrase indirectly raises a question about the inspiration of the epistle to the Galatians because there's an error here, plain and simple. Paul rebukes these people for turning to a different gospel. In the same breath, he corrects himself under the power of the Holy Spirit and writes **not that there is another one** (v. 7). "I can't believe you're turning to another gospel. Oh, but there isn't actually another gospel. There's only one gospel."

If you were to ask me to embrace the teaching of Rome today or the Judaizers of the first century, I would not be able to because neither one of them has a gospel. The gospel is good news, but there's no good news in Rome. There's no message of the free offer of grace or of justification by faith alone, in Christ alone, to the glory of God alone, to be found in Rome. You're not going to find it in Trier or in Aachen with Joseph's pants either.

If you told me that my salvation depends on my faith *and* my works, God's grace *and* my merit, Jesus' help *and* my response, I would not count that as good news. If you told me that if I die with the slightest blemish of sin on my soul, I would go not to heaven but rather to the place of purging, that the fires of purgatory would cleanse me until I have enough merit and righteousness to enter the kingdom of God, I would not receive that as good news. It would not be good news because I know how much sin there is in my life, and if I have to go to purgatory and become perfect before I can enter the kingdom of God, I will be in purgatory for a very long time. No, the gospel is the good news that the basis of my salvation is not my merit and is not my righteousness; rather, it is the righteousness of Christ freely imputed to all who put their trust in Him.

This was the issue in the sixteenth century during the Reformation. This was the issue in the first century. This has been the issue in every generation of people who think that they can add something of value and merit to effect their salvation. The only righteousness by which we can ever possibly be saved is an alien righteousness, a foreign righteousness, a righteousness that is apart from us. It is the righteousness of Jesus Christ. Paul says the Galatians **are turning to a different gospel—not that there is another one** (vv. 6–7). Did you get that? There is no other gospel. There's only one gospel. This statement defies political correctness. As soon as you affirm exclusivity, saying there's only one way to God, only one Savior, only one gospel, you fly in the face of political correctness and risk your reputation in the process. Paul doesn't hesitate. There is no other gospel.

But there are some who trouble you and want to distort the gospel of Christ (v. 7). To emphasize that there is only one message of salvation, Paul points out that there are some who **distort the gospel** by proclaiming another way to be saved. They have no truth to offer; all they can do is twist what God has revealed. So they take the gospel out of focus, blur it, confuse it. They allow the sharpness of the Word of God to be left clouded in vagueness and uncertainty.

But even if we or an angel from heaven should preach to you a gospel contrary to the one we preached to you, let him be accursed (v. 8). If John, Peter, James, Andrew, or an angel from heaven—anyone at all—tries to change the gospel and teach a different gospel than the one true gospel, Paul says, may God curse them. The word **accursed** translates the Greek word *anathēma*. This word has come directly into the English language and means anything that is unacceptable or opprobrious. The Roman Catholic Church responded to the Protestant Reformation at the Council of Trent in the middle of the sixteenth century, and there it defined its doctrine of justification. The Roman Catholic Church put a curse on all those who disagreed with its teaching, stating that anyone who holds to justification by faith alone is *anathema*. In the Roman Catholic Church, that anathema still stands.

Anytime somebody says to you, "God damn you," that's what anathema means. "May God put His curse on your head. May God send you to hell if you preach any other gospel than that which has come from His Word in the New Testament."

As we have said before, so now I say again: If anyone is preaching to you a gospel contrary to the one you received, let him be accursed (v. 9). Paul, when he wrote these words, was direct. He didn't care about being politically correct. What he said simply is "I don't care who it is, how much authority they have, how much esteem they have; if they preach any other gospel, may God curse that person." He's not satisfied to say it once. Repetition was a common way to emphasize a point in the Jewish literary tradition. It's as though Paul said to the Galatians, "I know you don't want to hear again what I said to you, but I say to you again: If anyone is preaching to you a gospel contrary to the one you received, let him be anathema, or damned by God." This is serious business. We don't negotiate or sugarcoat or distort the gospel. If we do, we invite nothing less than the curse of God on our heads. This is business that couldn't possibly be any more serious.

3

LOVE LINES
AND MAN-PLEASING

Galatians 1:10

For am I now seeking the approval of man, or of God? Or am I trying to please man? If I were still trying to please man, I would not be a servant of Christ.

I was teaching a senior-level class in philosophy at a particular university. In that class I had thirty students, all of whom finished in the top fifty in that year's graduating class. This was the crème de la crème. The subject of our study was epistemology, which is the science of how we know whatever it is that we know.

The point of my lecture that day was not to debate the concept of macro-evolution, but I used that idea to illustrate my concerns. I began by taking a poll, asking the students, "How many of you believe the idea of macroevolution—namely, that all life has come from a single cell?" Twenty-seven students, or 90 percent of the class, raised their hands.

I went to the blackboard, and I wrote on the board the numbers one through five. I said, "We don't have time today to go into all the ramifications of the concept of macroevolution, but what I'm interested in is for us to present at least five of the most compelling arguments by which you, as students, were persuaded of the truth of this particular viewpoint." I wrote number one, looked around the classroom, and said, "Somebody, please give me the arguments that have persuaded you of this theory." One young fellow raised his hand and stated that all life is composed of the same basic substances: amino acids, proteins, and so on. He went on to say the argument convinced him since a common substance means a common source. I thanked him for this. This young man went on to become a medical doctor and then later a Ph.D. in neuroscience at Harvard. He's a very bright fellow. I pointed out to him that the idea of a common substance's pointing to a common source is a *possible* inference from the data but not a *necessary* inference. After we spoke about the argument for a few moments, he granted that it was not a compelling argument for evolution in and of itself.

I said: "Fine. Let's go on to some other arguments, the ones that were persuasive to the rest of the class." I went to number two. An eerie silence along with mystified and bewildered looks greeted me. I said, "Come on, someone tell me what else has persuaded you of macroevolution." A student raised her hand and said, "That's what I was taught in biology class in high school and in college." I wrote down number two: "That's what they were taught in high school and college." I said, "What I want you to tell me is not where you learned this concept or from whom you've learned it, but what were the compelling arguments that you learned in high school and in college that convinced you of the truth of this premise?" I said, "Let's go on to number three." However, there was no number three. There was no number four. There was no number five.

For the most part, people are convinced by some authority they trust, and they believe something without examining the arguments in a critical way. We call these "love lines." We call them this because we tend to trust people we love and admire. If they say something to us, even without proving their assertion, we nevertheless take it on faith. You'll see that the vast majority of people who are Baptist are Baptist because they grew up in a Baptist family or those who are Methodist grew up in a Methodist family. They say: "That's the way I was raised. That's how I was born and reared. It was good enough for my father. It was good enough for my grandfather. Therefore, it's good enough for me." Whatever we were taught by someone we admire, a trusted teacher or parent, becomes the final recourse of our proof.

The problem that this tendency produces is a failure to examine those things that we hold with great tenacity. We hold on to things without really subjecting them to critical analysis. This is what Paul was facing among the Galatians. He was astonished that they had so quickly moved from what Paul had taught them with respect to the gospel. You recall what we've already read in the Apostle's statement in verse 9: "If anyone is preaching to you a gospel contrary to the one you received, let him be accursed."

Now, the question I ask is this: How is it possible that so many of these Galatians had been seduced by the Judaizing heresy, which teaches that to be saved, one has to maintain the law of the Old Testament? How is it that after hearing the beautiful gospel of Christ, of the finished work that He has performed in His atoning death, of a death made once for all, that anybody would move away from that glorious gospel? I think the answer is love lines.

You can hear the discussions among the Galatians: "Every year for forty years, I've gone to Jerusalem for Yom Kippur, for the Day of Atonement. I went through the rituals of sacrificing the bulls and the goats for my sins. Now this Apostle tells us we don't need to do that anymore? Everything has changed. Some person, Jesus, died once and for all, giving a perfect atonement. No, no. I like the tradition. I like trusting in the rituals of my faith and celebrating the Passover. Maybe Jesus thought it was nice in the upper room to change the liturgy of the Passover, but we've been doing this Passover the same way every year for centuries. My father did it, my grandfather did it, my great-grandfather did it, and I'm going to continue to do it as well."

These ceremonies were designed by God to point forward to the fulfillment of the person and work of Jesus Christ. However, once they were fulfilled in Him, the people didn't want to let them go. They wanted to rest their confidence in the tradition, in the sacred rituals and ceremonies they had performed for centuries. For them, it was not finished by Jesus.

There's an informal fallacy that we find constantly repeated in the world throughout the press and on TV. It's called the informal fallacy of the *argumentum ad populum*. This fallacy means an argument "to the populace" or "to the people." In simple terms, it's something like this: Sixty thousand people can't be wrong. You determine truth not only by love lines but by taking a poll. You count noses. You determine the truth on the basis of the majority view.

You see this argument when people want to do away with the electoral college and decide the presidency on the basis of the nationwide popular vote. The electoral college elects the president on the basis of electoral votes won, with each state being entitled to a number of electors equal to its congressional delegation (representatives plus senators). Why is there an electoral college? When the founding fathers founded this nation, they did not found it as a democracy. They deliberately made a decision against having a democracy and rather founded the United States as a republic.

If you ask people, "What's the difference between a republic and a democracy?" most people will not know the answer. Simply stated, the difference between a republic and a democracy is the difference between the rule of law and the rule of man, respectively. The founding fathers did not want to have a nation governed by the masses or by the majority. As Alexis de Tocqueville warned, you can easily have a tyranny of the majority.

A single ruler, a king, a monarch can tyrannize his people. A dictator can be a tyrant. An oligarchy can be tyrannical. A majority that votes by counting noses can tyrannize everyone else. That's why we have the Bill of Rights, which recognizes certain individual premises, privileges, and rights that are guaranteed for every single person. Even if three hundred million people vote against a particular right and only one person votes for it, that person is protected by the law of basic rights, which cannot be set aside by a majority vote.

We have a problem when truth is so often determined by polls. John Calvin made this comment: "Let us boldly despise the whole world." Now, did he mean that we should hate everybody in the world? No, what he meant is that ministers of the gospel, those who are entrusted to preach the Word of God, must learn how to shut their eyes.

We have a symbol in the U.S. Justice Department: it's Lady Justice, carrying a sword and scales. The thing that is so peculiar about Lady Justice is that she wears a blindfold. Why? She's following Calvin's sage advice in the juridical arena. Calvin was saying that justice must be blind; justice must not be distributed on the basis of people's standing or resources; rather, people are to be treated with fairness according to the law.

We know that all too often, Lady Justice peeks and checks out the polls to see who's for her and who's against her. Even the justices of the Supreme Court are extremely influenced by popular opinion. How else could you explain the Dred Scott decision? How else could you possibly explain *Roe v. Wade*? The error was that the most fundamental right of all, the right to life, was denied in *Roe v. Wade* because Lady Justice took off the blindfold and looked at the groups that were strongly and vehemently asserting their agendas.

Nothing is more irritating and intolerable to the status quo of the world with all its wisdom, power, and strength than the Word of God. By nature as humans, we despise the wisdom and principles of God's Word. By nature, we reject it. By nature, we vote against it.

When Paul addresses the crucial issue of justification by faith alone, he asks, **Am I now seeking the approval of man?** (v. 10). Seeking the approval of man and going with popular wisdom rather than against it was his nature. When he was persecuting the church violently and dragging Christians to prison, he received the applause of men who were encouraging his actions until the Son of God knocked him to the ground and blinded him, saying, "Saul, Saul, why are you persecuting me?" (Acts 9:4). Paul had heard the applause and cheers of men when he was attacking Christ. Paul asked, "Am I still going to count noses in Galatia to see what the popular view is there?"

The prophet Jeremiah writes, "O LORD, you have deceived me, and I was deceived" (Jer. 20:7). If there was ever an understatement, it was this. He then goes on to say, in effect: "You are stronger than I am and You have prevailed. I fought, but I lost. You beat me. I've become a laughingstock all the day. When I go and try to fulfill the task that You gave to me when You consecrated me from my youth to be a prophet and to speak Your Word, I didn't know that I would be subjected to public ridicule. I didn't know that every day when I put on my prophet's garment and I go into the public square, I would hear the jeers and the boos of the people. Everyone, not just a few, but everyone mocks me. Whenever I speak, I cry out the words that You told me to say: 'Violence and destruction are coming!' But the Word of the Lord has become for me a reproach and a derision all day long. I can't take it anymore. I didn't ask for this job. I'm going to turn in my prophet's card, hand in my resignation. I will speak no more in His name. But there is in my heart, as it were, a burning fire shut up in my bones and I can't stop."

The biggest problem that Jeremiah faced was the false prophets, and there were many. Each time Jeremiah warned the people of Jerusalem about the coming judgment of God, the false prophets drowned out his warnings, saying: "Don't listen to Jeremiah. God isn't angry. We have peace with God." It was what Luther called a carnal peace, but the people had itching ears. They didn't want to hear about God's anathema, about God's curse, or about God's judgment. They wanted good, happy news. God told Jeremiah: "Jeremiah, let the false prophet who has a dream tell his dream. If the people want to hear it, let the false prophets preach all they want; that's not your concern. Nevertheless, let the man of God preach the Word of God faithfully." This is exactly what the Apostle Paul was doing, and the Judaizers didn't want it.

For am I now seeking the approval of man, or of God? (v. 10). Paul adds a rhetorical question to the threat of the curse. He tells us elsewhere to try, as much as is in our power, to be at peace with all men, to try to get along with people (Rom. 12:18). We're not supposed to go out of our way to be obnoxious, to add scandal to the gospel. There's plenty of scandal already built in to the gospel. We don't need to add to it; nor are we allowed to subtract from it in order to please men.

The greatest theological crisis that I've ever been involved in was in the 1990s when a joint declaration came out between Roman Catholic leaders and evangelical leaders who were trying to have common cause to deal with issues like abortion and the sanctity of marriage and other things that we all agree on. However, they went beyond those common cause issues and declared a unity of faith in the gospel between advocates of the Council of Trent and so-called evangelicals. Some of my closest friends and closest coworkers were at the heart of this movement. I'd spoken with them, worked with them, taught them, prayed with them, and I now had to say no to them.

My own mentor, Dr. John Gerstner, called this document the most pernicious theological document ever produced in the twentieth century. It was a betrayal not only of the Reformation but of the gospel and of Christ Himself. I told the leaders of the movement behind this declaration my thoughts. Unlike Luther at Worms, I didn't have to stand alone. My experience was different from that of Athanasius, who in fighting the battle against the Arian heresy in the fourth century was exiled so many times for his fidelity to the gospel that he wore out his passport. For him, it was *Athanasius contra mundum*—"Athanasius against the world." I, however, didn't have to stand by myself. John MacArthur, D. James Kennedy, Michael S. Horton, John Ankerberg, James Montgomery Boice, and others stood firm with me. I wasn't standing by myself, but I did lose a number of friends and coworkers over that controversy, a controversy that continues to this very day.

I remember being in South Florida by myself at that time. I walked into an empty church at night and sat down. There was some subtle lighting inside and a Bible in a pew. I opened the Bible and read these words of the Apostle Paul: "If anyone is preaching to you a gospel contrary to the one you received, let him be accursed" (v. 9). Then I read verse 10: **For am I now seeking the approval of man, or of God? Or am I trying to please man? If I were still trying to please man, I would not be a servant of Christ**. That was a watershed moment in my life. When I walked out of that church, I knew there was no possible compromise on this issue. As I passed through the parking lot, I remembered the closing words in Luther's "A Mighty Fortress Is Our God": "Let goods and kindred go, this mortal life also. His kingdom is forever." I had to plug my ears and shut my eyes to the world's untruth if I wanted to be a servant of Christ.

Every one of us faces this kind of pressure, this kind of choice, at one time or another, when that which is popular will receive the applause of men. However, no matter how much applause we get from man, if we don't get the approval of God, it is nothing. If you want to be a Christian, you can't be a man-pleaser. Being a man-pleaser and a servant of Christ are two incompatible options. It's either/or. You please the Lord or you please your friends. If you have to cut every love line on this planet, get out your scissors for the sake of Jesus and for the sake of His kingdom.

4

PAUL'S AUTHORITY

Galatians 1:11–17

For I would have you know, brothers, that the gospel that was preached by me is not man's gospel. For I did not receive it from any man, nor was I taught it, but I received it through a revelation of Jesus Christ. For you have heard of my former life in Judaism, how I persecuted the church of God violently and tried to destroy it. And I was advancing in Judaism beyond many of my own age among my people, so extremely zealous was I for the traditions of my fathers. But when he who had set me apart before I was born, and who called me by his grace, was pleased to reveal his Son to me, in order that I might preach him among the Gentiles, I did not immediately consult with anyone; nor did I go up to Jerusalem to those who were apostles before me, but I went away into Arabia, and returned again to Damascus.

The Apostle proves that what he teaches is the truth of God and that what others say is a false gospel. He argues directly from the Bible, and he argues on the basis of logic to prove the same point. Either of these arguments would be sufficient to stand on its own foundation; it would be enough to say that he was an Apostle of God appointed by God to prove that what he taught had the imprimatur of God or that his sound arguments would be compelling no matter who preached them. So this is a doubly powerful refutation of the falsity of the Judaizers' message and the truth of the one the Apostle was preaching.

For I would have you know, brothers, that the gospel that was preached by me is not man's gospel. For I did not receive it from any man, nor was I taught it, but I received it through a revelation of Jesus Christ (vv. 11–12). This letter was written about twenty years after the Apostle's conversion on the road to Damascus. Everybody who read this letter knew exactly what Paul meant and believed implicitly that the message he had preached to them on other occasions was not of his own invention. He was not a false prophet who spelled out his own dreams; this was a man who was commissioned by heaven with the authority of God, and his gospel came not from him or from men or through men but from God by a revelation, an unveiling of God's great redemptive purpose in the gospel of His Son, Jesus.

He writes in a rather familiar fashion to the Galatians, whom, after all, he knew very well. He had been their pastor and their father in the faith; they loved him deeply, as he's going to remind them later. This is what makes the sudden change so extraordinary and surprising, as well as deadly. Here he's talking in a rather casual way: **For you have heard of my former life in Judaism, how I persecuted the church of God violently and tried to destroy it. And I was advancing in Judaism beyond many of my own age among my people, so extremely zealous was I for the traditions of my fathers** (vv. 13–14). In other words, the Apostle Paul was steeped in Judaism. He's refuting it now, and he's going to show precisely why he left Judaism and why the Galatians, who are reverting to what he had left, should not embrace it. Before he does that, he points out that he was the profoundest of sinners. After all, if Judaism is a false gospel, it is noteworthy that he was more steeped in it than any of the Galatians ever were.

But when he who had set me apart before I was born, and who called me by his grace, was pleased to reveal his Son to me, in order that I might preach him among the Gentiles, I did not immediately consult with anyone (vv. 15–16). I'm struck by that statement because Paul recognizes that God was setting him apart, even before he was born, by way of training him in the very error that he was here exposing and refuting. This background provided Paul with a deep experience of works-righteousness and the ability to recognize the Judaizing heresy for what it was—a return to Judaism and a rejection of the gospel—so when he recoils from the Judaizing heresy and repudiates it as a false gospel, you know that he knows what he's talking about. The Apostle is aware that from the moment of his birth, while he was still in his mother's womb, he was being trained by God; when he was circumcised at eight days, when he was reared in the rabbinic tradition, when he sat at Gamaliel's feet, when he became a rabbi among the rabbis and a Hebrew among the Hebrews, he was being trained by God. All that, mind you, was his training to be an Apostle of Jesus Christ, and God had purposed it all. God knew exactly what He was doing by putting Paul through this kind of preparation to be His Apostle.

Nor did I go up to Jerusalem to those who were apostles before me, but I went away into Arabia, and returned again to Damascus (v. 17). Paul's point is that he understands the message he speaks, from God Himself, with absolute authority. He didn't have any contact with the original Apostles for three years (v. 18). Therefore, no one could think that this was an importation of a Jerusalem gospel, that Paul sat at the Apostles' feet, or that he was just a Jewish convert whom these earlier Jewish convert Apostles had trained as a special emissary to the Gentile world because he showed such great promise. No, Paul immediately encountered the risen Jesus Christ on the Damascus Road, and he was immediately incommunicado, as it were, from the whole Apostolate. For three years, he went to seminary with God as his professor.

Three years is the usual duration of seminary training. I don't know whether God was trying to tell us something by the fact that when He trained His Apostle, He took three years. Nevertheless, I would certainly like to have attended that seminary where the only professor was God Himself.

5

PAUL IN JERUSALEM

Galatians 1:18–24

Then after three years I went up to Jerusalem to visit Cephas and remained with him fifteen days. But I saw none of the other apostles except James the Lord's brother. (In what I am writing to you, before God, I do not lie!) Then I went into the regions of Syria and Cilicia. And I was still unknown in person to the churches of Judea that are in Christ. They only were hearing it said, "He who used to persecute us is now preaching the faith he once tried to destroy." And they glorified God because of me.

The year 2017 was the five hundredth anniversary of the beginning of the Protestant Reformation, when Martin Luther nailed his Ninety-Five Theses on the Castle Church door in Wittenberg, Germany. When historians look back at this watershed moment and the movement it sparked, the question is this: What caused this tremendous schism in the Christian church? The almost unanimous answer is that there were two distinct causes for the Reformation: the material cause and the formal cause. This language regarding causality was used by the philosopher Aristotle and was then embraced by the medieval church and continues even to this day.

What do we mean by the material cause of the Reformation? In order to illustrate the meaning of that, let me give brief attention to a well-known poem composed by Clement Clarke Moore on the occasion of the celebration of Christmas. It begins with the familiar words "'Twas the night before Christmas, and all through the house, not a creature was stirring, not even a mouse. . . .

The children were nestled all snug in their beds; while visions of sugar plums danced in their heads."

Do you remember where the author writes, "Mamma in her 'kerchief, and I in my cap, had just settled down for a long winter's nap"? This is a picture of pure domestic tranquility. Everything was calm and peaceful that night. Instantly, everything changed. "When out on the lawn there arose such a clatter. I sprang from my bed to see what was the matter." What was the matter?

Santa Claus was the matter. The man in the poem looked out the window, and he saw a miniature sleigh and eight tiny reindeer. The question that arises from the poem is the same question that the historians asked about the Reformation. What was the matter? They were looking for the cause that provoked the issue of separation from Rome. The matter, simply put, was the gospel.

The matter was that during the centuries of the Middle Ages, the gospel had slowly been changed. Additional layers that didn't belong were slowly added to the gospel. The matter for the Reformation was the affirmation that Martin Luther made: that we are justified, as the gospel tells us, *sola fide*—by faith alone.

So often when we try to understand these things—Luther's protest and the controversy that ensued—Protestants tend to slander the Roman Catholic Church and draw a false dichotomy, saying: "Protestants believe that justification is by faith. The Roman Catholics believe that justification is by works." No, the Roman Catholic Church has made it abundantly clear that faith is a necessary condition for salvation, that grace is a necessary condition for salvation, and that Christ is a necessary condition for salvation.

So then, what was the matter? The problem was that the formula was changed by the Roman Catholic Church. It became faith plus works equals justification or, put in another way, grace plus merit equals justification. It became Christ plus me, working together, produces my salvation. In 1517, Luther stood up and said, "No, that's not the gospel."

Historians, using the language of Aristotle, say that the formal cause of the Reformation was a question of the issue of authority. When Luther posted the theses and made his protest, people said: "Luther, who do you think you are? You're standing alone against the historic teachings of the church." There occurred significant disputations with theologians and the Roman Catholic Church, particularly in Augsburg and Leipzig with Cardinal Cajetan of Rome and Johann Eck, the great sixteenth-century German theologian of the Roman Catholic Church.

In those debates, Luther was maneuvered to admit that he was standing against decisions that were made by popes and even by church councils. His defense was that the councils didn't always agree with each other and the popes contradicted each other. Luther's position was clear that his authority was God's Word. Thus, he affirmed in 1521 at the Diet of Worms: "Unless I am convinced by Scripture and plain reason, . . . my conscience is captive to the Word of God. I cannot and will not recant anything."

Sola Scriptura—Scripture alone as the Christian's final, infallible authority—was born along with *sola fide*. Thus, we see that the primary cause of the Reformation was the issue of the gospel, but looming just underneath the surface was the secondary cause, the question of authority.

Does that sound familiar? In Paul's letter to the Galatians, the Apostle was fighting a battle on two fronts. Two issues were burning at this period in early church history. Fifteen hundred years before Luther's confrontation with Rome, Paul faced the same question on the nature of the gospel. The material cause of Paul's writing to the Galatians was the gospel.

The Galatians had traded the gospel for something else. They had exchanged the gospel for another gospel, one that is not truly another gospel. So the Apostle said, "If anybody preaches any other gospel, even if it's an angel from heaven, let him be accursed." Let the anathema of God fall on him.

At the same time that Paul had to fight the battle for the gospel, he also had to battle the issue of his own authority, of his own credentials. The Galatians, who had rejected the gospel, said: "Who is Paul to say what the gospel is? We know better than the Apostle Paul." Paul had labored the point of his credentials as an Apostle called by Christ directly on the road to Damascus, and he labored the point that he had not received the gospel from men. It was not his desire to please men. He said, "If I please men, then I can't be a servant of Christ."

After three years I went up to Jerusalem (v. 18). Acts tells us that directly after Paul's conversion on the road to Damascus, Ananias was sent to see him, at which time he had his sight restored and was filled with the Holy Spirit (Acts 9:1–19). From there, he went to Arabia. It was three years later that Paul went to Jerusalem.

The point that Paul is making in rehearsing his history is that he did not learn the gospel or receive his call from Peter or from Andrew or from James or from John. He learned the gospel and received his call from God, from a direct revelation from Christ, not from any man.

In Matthew 16, Jesus and His disciples were in Caesarea Philippi, and He said to them, "Who do people say that the Son of Man is?" (v. 13). They gave various answers, and then Jesus looked at them and said, "But who do you say that I am?" (v. 15). Peter said, "You are the Christ, the Son of the living God" (v. 16). Jesus said in response, "Blessed are you, Simon Bar-Jonah! For flesh and blood has not revealed this to you, but my Father who is in heaven" (v. 17).

Jesus said to Peter, in effect: "You didn't learn the gospel from men any more than Moses received the law from men. Moses went to the holy mountain and received from the voice of God the commandments of the law." So stirring was that moment that Moses' face began to shine as he came down the mountain. It shone with such brilliance that the people begged him to cover it because the glory was too much for them to bear.

After three years, Paul **went up to Jerusalem to visit Cephas and remained with him fifteen days** (v. 18). Did Paul go up to Jerusalem to learn the gospel from Cephas (i.e., Peter)? No, he already knew the gospel. He learned the gospel from Jesus. Paul had already been preaching the gospel for three years.

But I saw none of the other apostles except James the Lord's brother. (In what I am writing to you, before God, I do not lie!) (vv. 19–20). Why does Paul say that? He swears an oath that he went to Jerusalem only to meet with Peter and to perhaps interview Peter regarding Jesus' life and teaching. But he was not there as Peter's student. He wasn't there to learn the gospel. He was emphasizing this to the Galatians who were challenging his Apostolic authority.

We are warned in Scripture not to swear by the earth or the altar or any human thing; rather, the only oath that is acceptable to God is one that is solemnly sworn by His power and presence. Why? If I swear something on my mother's grave, what good is that? My mother's grave can't see anything. If I swear on my mother's grave, and if I disobey what I've just said or if I lie, then what I've spoken can make no sanctions against me. My mother's grave is a place where we deposit her bones. It's powerless, impotent. Only God can ultimately judge the truthfulness of an oath. Paul is saying, "I'm vowing to you lest I lie and be exposed to the wrath of God, who enforces such vows."

I went into the regions of Syria and Cilicia. And I was still unknown in person to the churches of Judea that are in Christ (vv. 21–22). The churches in Judea had heard of Paul and knew him as the man who was casting Christians into prison and having them killed (see Acts 9:13–14). But something had changed. Paul finishes this portion of the letter by saying, **They only were hearing it said, "He who used to persecute us is now preaching the faith he once tried to destroy." And they glorified God because of me** (vv. 23–24).

What's the implication? "I started the church in Galatia. You knew me face-to-face. Rather than honor me, you vilified me. Rather than subjecting yourselves to the truth of the gospel that I gave to you by the authority invested in me by Jesus Christ, you had no respect for the gospel or for me." This was the formal cause of Paul's writing this letter of rebuke and correction to the Galatians.

I hear people say: "I don't care about doctrine. Doctrine divides. I have no creed but Christ." The Bible is almost 100 percent filled with doctrine. It's doctrine by which we live. It's doctrine by which we are redeemed. It is the gospel that is pure doctrine, that is a matter of life and death.

If you say you don't care about doctrine, what I hear you saying is this: "I don't care about the Word of God. I don't care about the gospel. I can have my own gospel, and you can have your gospel. Who cares what kind of a gospel you have?"

The Apostle Paul cared, Christ cares, and God, whose gospel it is, cares deeply. It is of utmost importance because doctrine is a matter of eternal life and death. Although, not every doctrine has the same gospel weight. There are doctrinal areas where we can disagree, and we can live in peace and harmony as Christians without dividing. However, there are core, central issues of gospel importance. These are the issues where, when there is a clatter, we need to jump to see what is the matter. The matter is doctrine—the doctrine of the gospel.

6

PAUL
AND CIRCUMCISION

Galatians 2:1–10

Then after fourteen years I went up again to Jerusalem with Barnabas, taking Titus along with me. I went up because of a revelation and set before them (though privately before those who seemed influential) the gospel that I proclaim among the Gentiles, in order to make sure I was not running or had not run in vain. But even Titus, who was with me, was not forced to be circumcised, though he was a Greek. Yet because of false brothers secretly brought in—who slipped in to spy out our freedom that we have in Christ Jesus, so that they might bring us into slavery—to them we did not yield in submission even for a moment, so that the truth of the gospel might be preserved for you. And from those who seemed to be influential (what they were makes no difference to me; God shows no partiality)—those, I say, who seemed influential added nothing to me. On the contrary, when they saw that I had been entrusted with the gospel to the uncircumcised, just as Peter had been entrusted with the gospel to the circumcised (for he who worked through Peter for his apostolic ministry to the circumcised worked also through me for mine to the Gentiles), and when James and Cephas and John, who seemed to be pillars, perceived the grace that was given to me, they gave the right hand of fellowship to Barnabas and me, that we should go to the Gentiles and they to the circumcised. Only, they asked us to remember the poor, the very thing I was eager to do.

P aul mentions here his concern with respect to the two issues that were present in the Galatian community: the material issue and the formal issue. The material issue about which Paul was concerned was the gospel itself. And the formal issue was Paul's authority. That authority was being undermined and challenged by some in the Galatian community. What was at stake was not a secondary issue or minor doctrine but the central issue, the core issue, of the gospel. Paul tells us, as he continues his defense of his Apostolic authority, of his making another trip to Jerusalem.

Then after fourteen years I went up again to Jerusalem (v. 1). Was it fourteen years after his first visit to Jerusalem or was it fourteen years after his conversion? Scholars continue to debate this point. We don't know to which time Paul is referring, whether it was the time that he was coming for the offerings from Antioch or the time of the Council of Jerusalem, which we read about in Acts 15.

I went up again to Jerusalem with Barnabas, taking Titus along with me. I went up because of a revelation and set before them (though privately before those who seemed influential) the gospel that I proclaim among the Gentiles, in order to make sure I was not running or had not run in vain (vv. 1–2). Paul was wanting to make certain that he was not preaching a different gospel from that which was revealed to the other Apostles. He wanted his readers to understand two things: that he didn't gain his authority from the Apostles and that he was preaching the same message, the same gospel, that they were.

But even Titus, who was with me, was not forced to be circumcised, though he was a Greek (v. 3). The Judaizers insisted on maintaining the ceremonial aspects of the Old Testament laws and particularly the ceremony of circumcision, insisting that a person could not be saved unless he was circumcised. So, for the purpose of giving an example, Paul brings with him an uncircumcised Gentile named Titus who would later become bishop of Crete, though he remained uncircumcised (see Titus 1:5).

This whole question of circumcision was of tremendous import to the nation of Israel. It was not a recent invention. When God established His covenant with Abraham and his seed, He commanded that the rite of circumcision be administered to everyone who was set apart as a member of the Jewish nation (Gen. 17). Circumcision was a cutting rite. It was the rite that established the Old Testament covenant and was the sign of that covenant. The covenant of circumcision that was made by God with Abraham was two thousand years old—not a recent innovation—and it was a tradition among the Jews.

We see the word *tradition* being used in different ways in the Scriptures, particularly in the teachings of Jesus in the New Testament where Jesus castigates the Pharisees for replacing the law of God with the traditions of men. Human tradition was interposed and interjected to supplant and to remove the law of God, and when the Pharisees were guilty of that, Jesus spoke out strongly against the godless activity of legalism, imposing laws that were not from God but from men.

Because of such rebukes from Jesus, we have the tendency to think that *tradition* must be a bad thing. The Apostle Paul, however, speaks not only of the traditions of men but of the word *paradosis*, which means that which is given over from one generation to the next (see, e.g., 2 Tim. 2:2). He speaks of a different tradition, the Apostolic tradition, which was not of human invention but was of divine ordination. So there are human customs and divine traditions. Any tradition that is given to us from God is a valuable tradition and is not one that is to be treated lightly.

The whole question of tradition is controversial. When people get together in any kind of community—and particularly in the church—there are certain ways of doing things that are so entrenched that people would balk if anybody ever tried to change them. If you try to change something in the liturgy or something in the form of a church activity, inevitably somebody is going to say, "But we've always done it this way."

One of the richest and most entertaining Broadway productions that I've seen is *Fiddler on the Roof*. It deals with the poignant travails of poor Tevye, whose three daughters, each in turn, challenge the deeply rooted tradition of the Russian Jews to marry only by family arrangement. Tevye's daughters challenge the tradition because they want to marry on the basis of love.

The image of the title of the play—a fiddler on the roof—was provocative. Playing the fiddle is not an easy task. I struggle to hold my violin on a level surface, but if you try fiddling on a roof, you will come crashing down from that roof and get hurt or killed. That's what Tevye was facing. He was trying to maintain a tradition that was being challenged, and it was as precarious as a fiddler trying to keep his balance while fiddling on a steeply pitched roof.

We follow customs, and some of them are good. Many churches have a custom that they stand when they read the Scriptures. Not every church follows that custom. It's rooted in an Old Testament practice that started when the law was rediscovered under the reform of King Josiah. The prophet and scribe Ezra had a platform built, and the people stood almost all day as the Scripture, the law, was read from the platform in their presence (see Neh. 8). They remained standing the whole time. That is, however, a custom not a commandment.

Circumcision was not a human custom or tradition. It was ordained by God and was a law delivered to Abraham and to his seed, a law that defined the identity of the people of God, the whole Jewish nation. Circumcision, where the foreskin of the male's flesh was cut off, signified two things. On the one hand, with this tradition that God instituted, He was saying, "I've taken this people, this nation, of all the nations of the world, and I have set them apart. I have cut them out from the rest of the world to have a unique relationship with them." The second part of the symbol, from the human aspect, signified the Jewish male saying to God, "If I disobey Your covenant, may I be cut off from Your presence and from Your grace just as the foreskin of my flesh has been cut off from me."

Circumcision pointed to the identity of the Jew both in a positive and in a negative sense, in terms of blessing and of cursing. How important was circumcision to the Jews? When David was a young boy, the giant Goliath came out morning and night for forty days and challenged the Jewish army in a loud voice. Goliath taunted them, saying, "Why have you come out to draw up for battle? Am I not a Philistine, and are you not servants of Saul? Choose a man for yourselves, and let him come down to me. If he is able to fight with me and kill me, then we will be your servants. But if I prevail against him and kill him, then you shall be our servants and serve us" (1 Sam. 17:8–9).

The Jews were paralyzed in fear. Nobody wanted to engage in combat with Goliath. Young David—visiting the troops because he was bringing food to his brothers—heard the challenge coming from the lips of Goliath and couldn't believe what he was hearing.

Notice how David responds to the situation and identifies Goliath: "Who is this uncircumcised Philistine, that he should defy the armies of the living God?" (1 Sam. 17:26). Circumcision had been the identity of the people of God for two thousand years.

Even though God commanded Abraham and his seed to be circumcised, Paul is now coming to the Galatian region as the Apostle of the Gentiles, saying, "You don't have to have to be circumcised." How can this be? The Galatians responded: "We've always been circumcised, and if a person wants to be a Jew, he can't be one and remain uncircumcised. If you're going to bring the gospel to the Gentiles as you've brought it here, then we insist, as the party of the Jews, that any convert to Judaism subject himself to circumcision."

Paul explains that he went to Jerusalem with Titus, an uncircumcised convert to Christianity, where he, Paul, consulted with the other Apostles to be sure that he was in accord with them regarding the gospel. Titus, though he was a Greek believer, was not required to be circumcised, according to Paul.

Before he was included in Paul's second missionary journey, Timothy, the product of a mixed marriage (his mother a Jew and his father a Gentile), was circumcised (see Acts 16:1–3). However, Paul did not require Titus to be circumcised. Why this seeming discrepancy? Paul said the Old Testament covenant was fulfilled when Jesus changed the terms of the covenant at the Last Supper. The new sign of the covenant was to be baptism, not circumcision. What, though, do we do with circumcision? Paul says, "Though it was obligatory for the Jew in the Old Testament and was a matter of *must*, it is now, with the change in the fulfillment of redemptive history, a matter of *may*." Such matters are called *adiaphora*—things indifferent—in the New Testament.

Paul labors the principle when he deals with the question of food offered to idols (see 1 Cor. 8). The Christian community knew that one of the practices of pagan worship was to offer food sacrifices to their deaf and dumb idols. After they offered it, the food that was left was taken to the marketplace and sold. Some in the Christian community said: "We can't eat that food. It has been a part of pagan worship. It's now tainted and unclean, and so it would be a sin for us to eat it."

Paul says in effect: "That food is just food. It doesn't change its nature just because a pagan used it in a religious ceremony. You can eat this food without having any concern about it. If you have this religious scruple, you're the weaker brother." However, Paul explains that if you care about your brother and his sensitivity when it comes to eating food that has been offered to idols, even though, in and of itself, it's a matter of indifference, you have the option of not eating food offered to idols. You don't *have* to eat that food that is offered. It's a matter of indifference, a matter of liberty. You are free to eat it if you want to, but for the sake of your weaker brother, you may refrain as well.

The difference is between *may* and *must*. He says that same thing about circumcision. "Now that the new covenant has arrived, you may continue with circumcision, just as I circumcised Timothy, but it's no longer a law. It's not obligatory. It's not binding on the Gentile convert to have to submit to circumcision. It's a matter of indifference. You *may*, but it's not a *must*."

Many people don't understand that difference. I know people who have been raised in strict Christian homes where they were taught from childhood that certain activities are sinful. People have added to the law of God, thinking that they are being obedient, and they condemn or forbid as harmful things that have nothing to do with the kingdom of God.

Sometimes, when people believe that something is sinful, they try to impose their belief as a universal law in the church. To that, Paul would say that while we are free to be sensitive and loving and care about the weaker brother, we never should submit to the tyranny of the weaker brother. We must never allow a human scruple to be elevated to the level of universal law in the church.

This is what was going on with the Galatians and their principle of circumcision. They wanted the *may* to be a *must*. Paul understands that it is a thing indifferent, a rich tradition that was there for a reason, but now that reason has been fulfilled by Christ. Continuing the old tradition is fine, but attempts to make it a requirement to enter the kingdom of God must be strongly resisted. So he says, **Because of false brothers secretly brought in—who slipped in to spy out our freedom that we have in Christ Jesus, so that they might bring us into slavery—to them we did not yield in submission even for a moment, so that the truth of the gospel might be preserved for you** (vv. 4–5).

Paul was all things to all men. When he was with the Jews, he dealt with the Jews as a Jew. When he was with the Gentiles, he dealt with them as the Gentiles in matters of indifference, but in matters of divine obligation, he would never submit himself to acts of tyranny and legalism that would destroy or cast a shadow on the gospel and the liberty that comes with the gospel. He talks about those who were **false brothers**. They were unconverted, but they had their formal relationship to Judaism, so they were fighting for this tyranny. They would spy out Paul's liberty, waiting for "gotcha" moments to say: "Aha! I saw you circumcise Timothy, and now you won't circumcise Titus. We got you, Paul, in your inconsistency."

Some people claim that calls to obey the law of God amount to legalism. However, legalism is when someone adds laws that God never prescribed. Legalism is when someone substitutes salvation by the works of the law for salvation by faith alone and by grace alone. Obedience to the law is not legalism. "If you love me," Jesus said, "you will keep my commandments" (John 14:15).

And from those who seemed to be influential (what they were makes no difference to me; God shows no partiality)—those, I say, who seemed influential added nothing to me. On the contrary, when they saw that I had been entrusted with the gospel to the uncircumcised, just as Peter had been entrusted with the gospel to the circumcised (for he who worked through Peter for his apostolic ministry to the circumcised worked also through me for mine to the Gentiles) (vv. 6–8). The Apostles were of one mind as they confirmed: "Paul, we recognize your call, your vocation. God has anointed you to be the Apostle to the Gentiles, and we are standing with you that you are not to require the Gentiles to be circumcised." Paul says to Peter and James and those who were ministering to the Jews, "Yes, and you are Apostles to Israel, and if you want to have them circumcised, that's fine, as long as it's not a law, as long as we understand that we both have a responsibility to declare the gospel in its purity, with all the freedom that is contained therein."

Paul concludes this passage by saying that they had all received the grace that had been given them: **And when James and Cephas and John, who seemed to be pillars, perceived the grace that was given to me, they gave the right hand of fellowship to Barnabas and me, that we should go to the Gentiles and they to the circumcised. Only, they asked us to remember the poor, the very thing I was eager to do** (vv. 9–10).

7

PAUL VERSUS PETER

Galatians 2:11–16

But when Cephas came to Antioch, I opposed him to his face, because he stood condemned. For before certain men came from James, he was eating with the Gentiles; but when they came he drew back and separated himself, fearing the circumcision party. And the rest of the Jews acted hypocritically along with him, so that even Barnabas was led astray by their hypocrisy. But when I saw that their conduct was not in step with the truth of the gospel, I said to Cephas before them all, "If you, though a Jew, live like a Gentile and not like a Jew, how can you force the Gentiles to live like Jews?"

We ourselves are Jews by birth and not Gentile sinners; yet we know that a person is not justified by works of the law but through faith in Jesus Christ, so we also have believed in Christ Jesus, in order to be justified by faith in Christ and not by works of the law, because by works of the law no one will be justified.

Paul's trip to Jerusalem recounted in 2:1–10 indicates that the Apostles were of one mind and the right hand of fellowship had been exchanged between Peter and Paul. These two were the titans of the early church, Peter principally as the Apostle to the Jews and Paul as the Apostle to the Gentiles. But suddenly a conflict arose between these two heroes of the faith, something you would never expect to read in sacred Scripture.

But when Cephas came to Antioch, I opposed him to his face, because he stood condemned (v. 11). Paul voiced his opposition to Peter not behind his back or through the rumor mill, but he spoke frankly, forthrightly, and directly to Peter. The opposition was not hidden or concealed from public view but was now made an open matter.

With respect to the ceremonial law and especially circumcision, Paul had behaved in different ways at different times with different people. He said that he became all things to all men. With respect to Timothy, he circumcised Timothy, but with respect to Barnabas, he refused to circumcise him. So, Paul says: "When I was with the Jews, I behaved like a Jew. When I was with the Gentiles, I was behaving like a Gentile." Why would Paul now find fault with Peter for doing the same thing? That's the difficulty of this particular text. Paul is rebuking Peter because Peter **stood condemned**. Why did he stand condemned?

For before certain men came from James, he was eating with the Gentiles; but when they came he drew back and separated himself, fearing the circumcision party (v. 12). When Paul became a Jew for the sake of the Jews and a Gentile for the sake of the Gentiles in matters that were indifferent, matters that were adiaphorous, Paul did just as he commanded us to do with those who had scruples about food offered to idols.

Paul's position was driven by charity; Peter's vacillation was not. It was motivated not by love or concern for the weaker brother but rather by intimidation and cowardice. Peter had learned at Cornelius' household through a vision that all foods were considered clean (Acts 10). God announced to Peter that the things that had been unclean in the Old Testament were now clean, and he was free to eat with the Gentiles whatever they were eating.

Peter sat down with the Gentiles and ate like a Gentile. What had been formerly declared unclean had now been declared clean by God. Peter rightly concluded he was free to eat with Gentiles. Previously, Jews wouldn't have had table fellowship with the Gentiles because Gentiles were considered unclean. Now Peter, being free and liberated by the Holy Spirit and by special revelation, could gather with Gentiles and eat with them without the requirement to eat only kosher food.

When a delegation sent by **the circumcision party**—that is, the Judaizers—came from Jerusalem to see what he was doing, Peter saw them coming and separated himself from fellowship with the Gentiles. Suddenly, he appeared as a strict dietary Jew out of fear of the Judaizers' response. Paul opposed Peter, saying: "This is dissembling. This is hypocrisy. You're not doing this for the sake of the gospel. You're doing it because you're afraid of the party of the circumcision." So, Paul rebuked Peter. The assumption that we can make from what we find in the rest of the Scriptures is that Peter accepted that rebuke and that the relationship between Paul and Peter was not destroyed. It was repaired, but not before Paul had to call him out publicly for his attempted deception.

And the rest of the Jews acted hypocritically along with him, so that even Barnabas was led astray by their hypocrisy. But when I saw that their conduct was not in step with the truth of the gospel, I said to Cephas before them all, "If you, though a Jew, live like a Gentile and not like a Jew, how can you force the Gentiles to live like Jews?" (vv. 13–14). The matter was even more serious than it first appeared, because not only was Peter guilty because of his fear of the circumcision party but the rest of the Jews acted hypocritically along with him. **Even Barnabas was led astray by their hypocrisy.** So Paul confronted Peter for his radical inconsistency in enjoying the freedom of the gospel while trying to deny that freedom to Gentiles.

We ourselves are Jews by birth and not Gentile sinners; yet we know that a person is not justified by works of the law but through faith in Jesus Christ, so we also have believed in Christ Jesus, in order to be justified by faith in Christ and not by works of the law, because by works of the law no one will be justified (vv. 15–16). In Romans 3:19–20, Paul says the same thing: "Now we know that whatever the law says it speaks to those who are under the law, so that every mouth may be stopped, and the whole world may be held accountable to God. For by works of law no human being will be justified in his sight, since through the law comes knowledge of sin." He speaks the same words here to the Galatians that he had previously spoken to the Romans.

No one means nobody. No one could ever possibly be justified by **works of the law**. Paul is laboring this whole doctrine of the gospel of justification by faith alone. The gospel is simple. The doctrine of justification by faith alone does not require a Ph.D. in theology to understand it. A six-year-old child can understand it. To get it in your head is one thing; to get it in the bloodstream where you live on the basis of justification by faith alone is so hard that even the Apostle Peter was caving in to this Judaizing heresy.

Many years ago, I was a minister in Cincinnati, where I served as minister of evangelism. I trained people in the method of evangelism started by D. James Kennedy. The Evangelism Explosion method of evangelism uses two diagnostic questions.

The first question is "Have you come to the place in your thinking where you know for sure that when you die, you're going to go to heaven?" The genius of this plan is that it starts with a question to which people feel comfortable answering no. People are not only willing to say they are not sure that they will go to heaven, but they are suspicious of anybody who answers in the affirmative, certain they are going to heaven at death.

The second question is "If you were to die tonight and stand before God and He asked you, 'Why should I let you into My kingdom?' what would you say?" We kept records of people's answers to that question. Ninety percent of the people responded with some kind of answer involving works-based righteousness. They said things like this: "I've tried to live a good life. I tried not to harm anybody. I didn't commit any criminal felonies or anything like that. So, I think that to the best of my ability, I have done what God wants me to do. That's why I think God ought to let me into His heaven."

We mentioned in a previous chapter that many people have a caricature of the Roman Catholic Church. They think that Protestants believe in justification by faith and Roman Catholics believe in justification by works. That's not only not true; it's slanderous to Roman Catholics. I don't know of any Roman Catholic theologian who wouldn't say that justification is by faith.

In the sixteenth century, the Roman Catholic authorities carrying out the Counter-Reformation in response to the Reformation assembled in the Italian city of Trent. At the Council of Trent, the Roman Catholic Church gave its definitive dogma, its formal definition, of how justification occurs. At the beginning of the exposition of the doctrine of justification, they labored the point that justification is by faith. They said three things about faith as it relates to justification: faith is necessary for justification because, in the first place, it is the initiation for justification, the *initium*; second, it's the foundation of justification, the *fundamentum*; and third, it's the root of justification, the *radix*. So, faith is the initiation, the foundation, and the root of justification.

The dispute in the sixteenth century wasn't whether justification is by faith. It was the same issue that was present in the Galatian church. The question was, Is justification by faith *alone*, or is it justification by faith plus something else—namely, the works of the law? The Roman Catholic Church talked about saving faith and said a person must have it, but that authentic saving faith, even if you have it, doesn't guarantee justification.

The Roman Catholic Church claims that a person can have faith as the initiation, as the foundation, and as the root of his justification but can still not be justified. A person can have saving faith and commit mortal sin and go to hell and spend eternity there. Or a person can have saving faith and go through the sacrament of penance, the so-called second plank of justification for those who make shipwreck of their souls. However, even if the person's status of justification is restored, if there is one blemish on the person's soul when he dies, he will not go to heaven. Rather, he will go to purgatory.

The Roman Catholic Church claims that only a handful of people in the history of the church have gone straight to heaven at death and that those few had more merit than they needed to get there. Their merit was deposited in the "treasury of merit." That was what the indulgence controversy was about in the sixteenth century; it was what sparked Martin Luther's protest. The issue was whether justification is by faith alone or if it is by faith plus something else. In the sacrament of penance, to be restored to a state of justification, one must do works of satisfaction to earn *meritum de congruo*, congruous merit. This is not merit that's good enough that it requires God to justify you but merit that makes it fitting or congruous for God to justify you. You have to have those works to be justified.

Protestants believe that you must have works as the fruit of your justification, as the proof of your justification, as the evidence of your justification. Those works that evidence a person's justification don't count at all toward his justification. They don't *cause* one's justification. The instrumental cause of justification is faith and faith alone. This is the dispute. This is what it's all about.

We also have believed in Christ Jesus, in order to be justified by faith in Christ and not by works of the law, because by works of the law no one will be justified (v. 16). I don't care how high your stack of good works is; it's not high enough or good enough for you to secure justification in the sight of God.

The only One whose works are good enough for justification is Jesus. That's why you have to have Jesus—because your works aren't good enough. You can work as hard as you can from now until kingdom come, and when that kingdom comes, if all you have are your works, you will perish forever. If you go back to works and if you believe in Christ, but you're turning away from the gospel, you have no savior left.

I've heard people say about the sixteenth-century Reformation that the whole thing was a misunderstanding, that it was a tempest in a teapot, that the whole thing was overdone over one little word: *alone*. Luther said on the contrary that the doctrine of justification is the article on which the church stands or falls. In effect, Paul was saying the same thing to Peter—that justification comes down to trusting in Christ and His righteousness, which is given or transferred to all who believe, rather than striving to obtain a righteousness of our own through adherence to the law. Luther called the justifying righteousness of Christ a *justitia alienum*, a foreign righteousness. It's not our own. It is, as Luther said, a righteousness that is *extra nos*, outside of us.

The righteousness by which we are justified is an alien righteousness. It's not a righteousness that we possess. It is not something that we gain or that we merit. Rome said, in the sixth session of the Council of Trent, that until or unless, with the help of grace, with the help of Jesus, with the help of faith, you finally come to the place in your life where true righteousness inheres within you, you will not be justified. God will never declare you just until or unless you really are just. *Inherent* is the word that is used by the theologians in Trent, a word that is still on the books today and is still maintained as vigorously as it ever was. The Roman Catholic Catechism of the 1990s teaches that a person must be "inherently" righteous or God won't pronounce a person righteous. To say otherwise, to say that God can pronounce someone righteous who is not actually, inherently righteous, would be a legal fiction, a lie. God would be saying you are righteous when you are not.

That's why Luther responded with another Latin phrase, *simul justus et peccator*, meaning "at the same time righteous and sinner." I am righteous by God's granting me the righteousness of Christ, but in and of myself, I'm still a sinner. If I have to wait until I'm sinless or for purgatory to remove every blemish from my soul, it would take a long time to get to be with my Savior.

If I believed that I had to do good works to get into the kingdom of God, I would be in utter despair. That's not the gospel. To think that you must have works to be justified destroys the gospel. By works of the law no one will be justified. The law has already labored that point. If anybody tells you another gospel—the pope, an angel from heaven, Peter, Barnabas, Silas, or even Paul—what you're hearing is not the gospel. It's bad news, not good news.

The good news is that "the righteous shall live by faith" (Gal. 3:11). That is, the righteous shall live by trust, trusting in the One who was righteous, who did fulfill the law, who kept every jot and tittle of the law. Jesus fulfilled the law and achieved perfect righteousness not for Himself, not so that He could qualify for salvation, but for you and for me. Jesus is my righteousness, and if you are a Christian, Jesus is your righteousness.

8

CRUCIFIED
WITH CHRIST

Galatians 2:17–21

But if, in our endeavor to be justified in Christ, we too were found to be sinners, is Christ then a servant of sin? Certainly not! For if I rebuild what I tore down, I prove myself to be a transgressor. For through the law I died to the law, so that I might live to God. I have been crucified with Christ. It is no longer I who live, but Christ who lives in me. And the life I now live in the flesh I live by faith in the Son of God, who loved me and gave himself for me. I do not nullify the grace of God, for if righteousness were through the law, then Christ died for no purpose.

This portion of the letter to the Galatians is not an easy one to expound. In fact, it's difficult and weighty, but nevertheless it is of extreme importance that we understand what the Apostle is teaching here and that we embrace it fully for the glory of God and for our salvation.

Several years ago, I was involved in a discussion with certain Christian leaders behind closed doors. The discussion was focused on a serious matter confronting the church and a contested issue that brought severe controversy even to those who had formerly been in agreement with respect to the evangelical faith. But in the midst of this discussion, I asked one of the people present, "Do you believe that the doctrine of *sola fide*, or justification by faith alone, is *essential* to the gospel?" He listened to the question, paused for a second, and

then replied, "I believe that justification by faith alone is *central* to the gospel."
I said to him—I hope politely and not sternly—"Sir, that's not the question I
asked you. I didn't ask you if justification by faith alone is *central* to the gospel.
I asked you, is it *essential* to the gospel?" Again, he looked at me and said, "I
believe that justification by faith alone is *central* to the gospel."

I thought I had been clear in my question, but once again I asked: "Sir, I'm
not asking you if justification by faith alone is *central*. I'm asking you if it is
essential, so that without justification by faith alone, you don't have the gospel."
He thought for a second, looked at me and replied, "I believe that justification
by faith alone is *central* to the gospel." At that point, I gave up the inquiry.

The reason I was asking the question of this gentleman was that when
dealing with the gospel, there is often difficulty in defining what the gospel
is. There are two aspects of the gospel. First, there is the objective meaning of
the gospel, and it has to do with the person and the work of Jesus Christ. The
gospel at its core is Christ.

But as Paul in his letter to the Galatians and elsewhere in Romans and Ephesians points out, the benefits of the objective work accomplished on our behalf
by Jesus can be gained by us only through the medium of faith. So, when we
speak about justification by faith alone, we're talking about how an individual
benefits from or appropriates the work of Christ for himself. It's at this point
that the question of the subjective side of justification by faith alone arises.
What Paul is getting at initially in this portion of the epistle is the inseparable
relationship between Christ, as the objective content of the gospel, and faith,
as the subjective means by which we receive Christ and our salvation. You can
distinguish between our faith and the work of Jesus Christ, but the gospel must
include both elements if it is to be the gospel.

Previously, we considered the difference between the material cause and the
formal cause of the sixteenth-century Protestant Reformation. We saw that the
language of the medieval church in this regard had been borrowed from the philosophy of Aristotle when he made the distinction between material and formal
causes. Let's consider this further. When Aristotle was dealing with causality,
he was trying to understand some of the mysteries associated with motion and
particularly the movement that we call change. Perhaps the most distinctive
characteristic that makes us different from God is that we are mutable. God is
immutable, and we are not. God never changes. He's the same yesterday, today,
and forever, whereas we, as His creatures, are always changing. Every second, we're
changing. The most common characteristic of our creatureliness is mutability.
We grow old. We become sick. Hopefully, we become healthy again. But, we
are all the time changing.

When Aristotle was contemplating mutability, he was asking, What causes change to come about? He came up with a series of distinctions about causality, including material causes and formal causes. I previously mentioned only those two, but he listed several others (the efficient cause, the final cause, and the instrumental cause). In Aristotle's analogy of causality, he gave an example of a sculptor who is making a statue. Aristotle said there's the material cause—the material of which the statue is made; the formal cause—the blueprint that he uses; and so on. Then he came to a critical discussion regarding the instrumental cause. The instrumental cause is the tool that is used to change a block of stone and turn it into a statue. The sculptor doesn't stand in front of that block of stone and say, "Abracadabra," and wait for the stone to turn into a statue; nor does he wait for chance, as many of our naturalist friends would suggest, for that stone to become a statue.

Aristotle said that if there is to be a change, an instrument has to be used by the sculptor as an instrument of change, so he called that cause the instrumental cause. This whole sixteenth-century issue came to the fore with respect to salvation. The debate between the Reformers and the Roman Catholic Church focused in part on the instrumental cause of our justification. Rome answered it this way: the instrumental cause, the means by which we are moved from the state of being unsaved and unjustified to the state of grace and being justified is the sacrament of baptism and (secondarily) the sacrament of penance. The Protestant Reformers said no, we're not moved from sin and damnation to salvation by the instrument of the sacraments; we are moved by the sole instrument of justification, which is faith. The Reformers were willing to die for the affirmation that the only instrument by which we are changed from unsaved to saved is faith and faith alone. This is what the whole battle was about in the sixteenth century and in first-century Galatia.

The Galatians, under the influence of the Judaizing heresy, were insisting that the only way to be saved or to be justified is through the instrumental cause of faith plus the instrumental cause of works. This was the same issue that was confronting the church during the sixteenth-century Reformation. At the time of the Reformation, Martin Luther, John Calvin, and the other Reformers faced a serious ethical charge and an ethical danger that had to do with the relationship of faith and works. The Roman Catholic authorities insisted that teaching justification by faith alone, apart from works, would lead to licentiousness or unholy living. Along similar lines, we talk today of easy-believism or cheap grace. This is when people say: "We're justified by faith alone not by works; therefore, we can live as godlessly as we want to. We can live constantly in sin. We can be carnal Christians, but if we believe in Jesus, that's all it takes and we'll be saved. Works have nothing to do with our salvation."

On the contrary, the doctrine of justification by faith alone means that we are justified by faith *unto* good works. Luther said, "We're justified by faith alone but not by faith that is alone." James writes, "Faith by itself, if it does not have works, is dead" (James 2:17). It's not real; it's a dead faith. Luther said saving faith is a *fides viva*, an alive faith, a living faith, a faith that will always and everywhere, if it's genuine, yield and produce good works and obedience to God.

The cardinal heresy of antinomianism is saying that we are so free from the law that we can have faith and live as lawlessly as we want and still be justified. That's the danger, and that's what the Galatians were hearing. They were thinking, "If we do away with the law, if we're simply justified by faith, then that means that we can be godless and still be saved, and that can't be right." The Roman Catholic Church was hearing the same thing in the sixteenth century from Martin Luther. Luther said, "You're justified by faith alone." They said, "Does that mean you can have faith and live as godlessly as you want?" Luther was not advocating godlessness, and the last thing he wanted was lawlessness. Here in Galatians, the Apostle Paul is not advocating lawlessness in the sense of disobedience, but rather he's trying to make this distinction: we are saved *unto* good works but not *by* our good works. Again, if you have no good works, that's proof that you don't have any faith. If you don't have any faith, you don't have any justification. But if you have true faith, you're justified, and then the works follow.

But if, in our endeavor to be justified in Christ, we too were found to be sinners, is Christ then a servant of sin? (v. 17). If I believe that I'm justified by faith alone and I still sin, what does that mean? Let me back up. I don't know that every person I meet is justified, but I do know one thing about everybody I come across: I know that every single person is a sinner. You may be a *justified* sinner or an *unjustified* sinner. I can't read your heart. We previously mentioned Luther's formula *simul justus et peccator*—"at the same time just and sinner." I am justified on the basis of the imputation of the righteousness of Christ by faith to me, but if God looks at me as I am, He will see a sinner. If He sees the most faithful servant in the vineyard of Jesus Christ, be it Peter or Paul or anybody else, He will immediately see that the person is a sinner.

If I say that I'm justified by Christ, which is what I mean when I say I'm justified by faith alone, and I'm still a sinner, what does that mean? It must mean that Jesus, rather than saving me from sin, is the cause of my sin. He is the minister of my sin and the agent of my sin. This is the question at hand: Doesn't it follow that if you're justified by Christ and not by the works of the law, then that must mean that Christ is another Moses who brings us back into the law again and leads us into sin? Paul is asking this as a rhetorical question, but he doesn't leave us without a clear answer.

Paul answers his own question in the same way that he responds to the Romans when dealing with the matter of sin's being met with God's abounding grace. Some may conclude that if when we sin abundantly, we get abundant grace, so let's really go on sinning so that grace may abound. Paul asks in Romans 6:1, "Are we to continue in sin that grace may abound?" He responds by saying, "By no means!" (Rom. 6:2), a phrase that is so emphatic that it might be translated "God forbid!" He tells them not to even think about it or for a second imagine that Jesus Christ is a minister of sin. This is the last conclusion we should possibly come to from the gospel of Jesus Christ. Christ is not the minister of sin. He is the minister of grace. But, if we don't believe that our salvation is by grace alone and we want to add the necessity of works to it, then once again we're under the law and will be slain by the law, and Christ would become a new Moses and a new mediator of sin.

Certainly not! For if I rebuild what I tore down, I prove myself to be a transgressor. For through the law I died to the law, so that I might live to God (v. 18). The Judaizers expected to be saved by the law as they sought to obey it alongside having faith in Christ. But Paul responds that the same law identifies sin and awakens the flesh to do more evil. Our works cannot justify us, so it is fruitless to lean on them for our righteousness. In fact, doing so only increases sin, as the law is powerless to save and can only curse us for our unrighteousness.

This was Luther's existential problem. He spent hours in confession every day because every time he read the law of God, he felt condemned by the law. He said, "You ask me if I love God, but sometimes I hate Him." In another place, he expressed a similar sentiment: "To the gallows with Moses. I don't want to hear about Moses. Every time I look at the law of God, I'm destroyed because I know that I don't keep the law." However, when you hear the gospel, which is not the law, and know that you are saved freely, not on the basis of your obedience of the law but on the basis of your faith in Christ, who perfectly obeyed the law, who did what you and I cannot do and will never be able to do—live a life of perfect righteousness—that is good news. The good news is that we don't have to keep the law to be saved.

There are, however, good uses for the law that we'll explore later. Paul never says the law is worthless. He says the law is still good and holy. One of the most important functions of the law is to slay us, because the law reveals the perfection of God; the law is like a mirror. When I look into the mirror of the law, what is the image that stares back at me? It is the image of a sinner. I don't obey the law. I never obey the law. The law says to love the Lord your God with all your heart and all your mind and all your strength, and I haven't loved the Lord my God with all my heart for one second in my life. Not a single second have I ever loved God with all my mind, and neither have you.

I look in that mirror, and all it shows is the ugliness of my sin. Paul says: "The law is like a schoolmaster that drives us to Christ. The law scolds me and drives me to a Savior who alone can save me." So Paul says in effect: "When I discovered the gospel, the law died. I didn't die; the law died in terms of its power of condemnation over me." This is why Paul can now say: "Who shall bring any charge against God's elect? It is God who justifies" (Rom. 8:33). So, Paul acknowledges: "When I died to the law in order that I might live to God, I didn't reject the law so that I could be lawless. I learned that through the law, I can never be justified. The only way I can be free to live for God is if I let the law die." Paul is saying to the Galatians, in effect, "Do you want to raise the law from the dead and add it to salvation? Do you want to make Christ the new minister of sin?"

For if I rebuild what I tore down, I prove myself to be a transgressor. For through the law I died to the law, so that I might live to God. I have been crucified with Christ. It is no longer I who live, but Christ who lives in me (vv. 18–20). Paul doesn't mean that he added anything to the benefits of the crucifixion of Christ. Paul doesn't say that his own crucifixion was the grounds of the atonement of his sins. He's saying, "When my Savior died, I died with Him." The old Paul, the old sinner, died with Christ.

Likewise, when he says, **It is no longer I who live**, it doesn't mean that he's physically dead. He says, **But Christ who lives in me.** I am united through faith by the Holy Spirit with Christ and with His death, His sacrifice, His atonement. I am in Christ. Christ is in me so that the moment I put my trust in Christ and in Christ alone, my identity changed forever, and the instrument by which that change took place was faith and faith alone.

And the life I now live in the flesh I live by faith in the Son of God, who loved me and gave himself for me. I do not nullify the grace of God, for if righteousness were through the law, then Christ died for no purpose (vv. 20–21). Paul is saying it would have been a futile sacrifice and that Christ would have died in vain. Paul pleads: "Is that what you want, O foolish Galatians? Do you want to come under the law again? Don't you realize that through the life and death of Jesus Christ, through the gospel you received by faith, you vitiate it all if you go back to the law and to works? You'll have no destiny other than perdition. You will have no hope." Do you see why Paul is so passionate about this? You can't start by faith and then add even one little detail to it.

I said previously that the Roman Catholic Church is slandered when we say, "We believe in justification by faith and they believe in justification by works" or "We believe in justification by grace and they believe in justification by merit." That's not really true because Rome has labored the point that faith is a necessary ingredient to be saved, so it's not true to say that they believe in justification by works. Or is it?

The minute you add any works to faith, you're saying that in the final analysis faith isn't enough. What decides your fate ultimately and eternally is what works you do. This is exactly what Paul is saying to the Galatians. If you want to rest at all on your works, if you want to add works as an addition to faith, you've destroyed your faith. You have destroyed the gospel. You have no gospel. All you have is the law that will condemn you.

9

O FOOLISH GALATIANS

Galatians 3:1–9

༄༅༅༅

O foolish Galatians! Who has bewitched you? It was before your eyes that Jesus Christ was publicly portrayed as crucified. Let me ask you only this: Did you receive the Spirit by works of the law or by hearing with faith? Are you so foolish? Having begun by the Spirit, are you now being perfected by the flesh? Did you suffer so many things in vain—if indeed it was in vain? Does he who supplies the Spirit to you and works miracles among you do so by works of the law, or by hearing with faith—just as Abraham "believed God, and it was counted to him as righteousness"?

Know then that it is those of faith who are the sons of Abraham. And the Scripture, foreseeing that God would justify the Gentiles by faith, preached the gospel beforehand to Abraham, saying, "In you shall all the nations be blessed." So then, those who are of faith are blessed along with Abraham, the man of faith.

The epistle of Galatians is uncharacteristic of the Apostle Paul. He was exercised by the reports he received from the Galatian church, that they had quickly departed from the purity of the gospel and were being seduced by false teachers in their midst. This was a most serious matter—the distortion of the very gospel. Instead of rehearsing any positive things that he has heard about the Galatians or how he is praying for them, as we read in his other epistles, here we find a strident tone. You can sense the Apostle Paul was disturbed and distressed in his spirit by the news of what was going on among the Galatian believers.

In chapter 3 it seems like he unleashed everything on the Galatians and held nothing back. He doesn't say, "Oh, gentle and beloved congregation, wonderful sheep of Jesus." He says: **O foolish Galatians! Who has bewitched you?** (v. 1).

Paul tells the Galatians that there's something wrong with their thinking. Most of the translators use the term **foolish** to try to capture the sense of what the Apostle is saying. When the Bible speaks of foolishness, it's not just speaking about a learning disability; rather, there is a strong moral element contained in the concept of foolishness.

When God came to Jeremiah and called him to be His spokesman, God put His words in Jeremiah's mouth and told him that He wanted Jeremiah to make an announcement to the people of Judah (see Jer. 1). That announcement was of God's coming judgment on the nation of Judah. In the fourth chapter, God says through the lips of the prophet, "For my people are foolish; they know me not; they are stupid children; they have no understanding. They are 'wise'—in doing evil! But how to do good they know not" (Jer. 4:22).

What an indictment God gives against the people of Judah through the prophet Jeremiah. Jesus spoke similarly to the people of His day, saying, "Then are you also without understanding? Do you not see that whatever goes into a person from outside cannot defile him, since it enters not his heart but his stomach, and is expelled?" (Mark 7:18–19). Then He goes on to say, "What comes out of a person is what defiles him. For from within, out of the heart of man, come evil thoughts" (Mark 7:20–21). Jesus gives a list of the gross and heinous sins that are born in the heart of fallen humanity: "evil thoughts, sexual immorality, theft, murder, adultery, coveting, wickedness, deceit, sensuality, envy, slander, pride, foolishness" (Mark 7:21–22). In God's eyes, foolishness is a grievous sin, a moral failing.

Why is unbelief not just foolish but immoral? Because, as Paul tells us in Romans, God has clearly revealed Himself to every human being. No one has to grope in the dark or use his intellect to find some glimpse of the existence of God. Rather, through nature, God reveals Himself so manifestly, so clearly, that everyone who claims to be an atheist is without excuse.

When people say, "I'm not an atheist; I'm an agnostic," I say, "That's worse." Or they say: "I'm not a militant atheist. I'm not on a crusade to do away with the existence of God and destroy religion. I just don't think there's enough evidence to make a decision one way or the other. Or the reason that I won't affirm the existence of God is because of insufficient knowledge." Who is at fault for someone's being an agnostic? Who is being blamed for this lack of knowledge? People who make such remarks are blaming God.

The Bible tells us in Romans that everyone knows that God exists. He is the perfect teacher and has revealed Himself plainly. Scripture says that is why the judgment on atheism is the judgment of foolishness and has a moral quality associated with it. In the Wisdom Literature of the Old Testament we are told, "The fear of the LORD is the beginning of wisdom" (Prov. 9:10). By contrast, what is the beginning of foolishness? The failure to hold God in reverence and to adore Him.

The foolishness that Paul speaks of, this distortion of the truth, is an expression of fallen humanity, an expression of sinfulness. It is utterly foolish not to listen to God, the most sure and positive source of truth that can be found anywhere in the universe.

I have seen the bumper sticker that reads, "God said it, I believe it, that settles it." That's not correct. Settling the truth of God doesn't require my belief or my assent. We need to eliminate the middleman. God says it; that settles it. It doesn't matter whether you believe or if I believe. If it's spoken by the Lord God omnipotent, the One who is omniscient, the debate is over.

Paul is just getting warmed up with his distress with the Galatians. **O foolish Galatians!** Then he raises a question that I have found puzzling for many years. Paul asks, **Who has bewitched you?**

We live in a time when we use language of bewitchment, but we don't believe in witches or goblins or things that go bump in the night. We don't believe that people really have the power to mesmerize others and actually delude their minds into thinking that they are bewitched. What does the Bible say about sorcery, about witchcraft, about necromancy? These are gross and heinous crimes according to God. He will not tolerate the presence of necromancers or sorcerers or magicians, people who practice the black arts. God won't permit them to live in the land. In fact, He will punish the whole nation if sorcery is tolerated.

You get the idea that there's no real power in sorcery, that any kind of alleged witchcraft has to be legerdemain, sleight of hand, a kind of magic that we are entertained by. We don't believe that people are doing miraculous things by supernatural power. We have been so influenced by the philosophy of naturalism that we don't believe that anybody could possibly have the power of bewitching other people.

When we come to this text, we think that Paul is speaking metaphorically, that he couldn't seriously be entertaining the idea that there's such a reality as witchcraft. I disagree. I read this text and think that the Apostle is in fact thinking there is such a thing. It's prohibited; it's condemned; it's absolutely wicked and evil but nevertheless real. When Paul asks, **Who has bewitched you?** I don't think that Paul has in mind something like the Old Testament witch of En-dor (see 1 Sam. 28) so much as the supreme deceiver.

Scripture teaches us that Satan is not just the tempter or the accuser but that he also is the deceiver, the one who muddles people's thinking, creating opportunity for their minds to be given over to the darkness because he is "the prince of the power of the air" (Eph. 2:2). In fact, when Jesus taught His disciples how to pray, He likely didn't teach them what many English translations say: "Lead us not into temptation, but deliver us from evil" (Matt. 6:13). In Greek, the word we have translated as "evil" can just as easily be translated as "the evil one."

Jesus tells His people that there is a devil in the world. Satan is real. Every page of the Scriptures communicates this supernatural reality—that this fallen angel, the leader of all those in the demonic realm, is Satan the liar, the deceiver, the evil one par excellence. There are few people today who even believe in the existence of Satan. We've been conditioned by naturalism to assume that the natural realm is all there is.

My professor at the Free University in Amsterdam said, "Beloved, if there is no demonology, there can be no theology." The same God who reveals Himself in sacred Scripture reveals also that evil exists in the person of Satan. Satan is stronger than you and I, but don't ever make the dualistic error of thinking that Satan is equal to God.

We are warned against lying signs and wonders, false miracles performed by Satan. What does Scripture mean when it speaks of lying signs and wonders? Are they real miracles that are being used in the service of evil? No, they are events that seem to be miracles externally, that have some of the visible characteristics of miracles, but they are *lying* miracles. They're false, phony, fake. The magicians of Egypt in Pharaoh's court performed lying signs and wonders in league with Satan. Satan's signs and wonders are always counterfeit, though they are nevertheless powerfully deceptive.

It's the same thing with angels. We may not see them, but they are active. Remember 2 Kings 6 when Elisha was alone with his servant and the servant saw that they were completely surrounded by the chariots of their enemies? "The servant said, 'Alas, my master! What shall we do?' He [Elisha] said, 'Do not be afraid, for those who are with us are more than those who are with them'" (2 Kings 6:15–16).

Elisha prayed for his servant and asked, "O LORD, please open his eyes that he may see" (2 Kings 6:17). Elisha was essentially asking the Lord to allow the servant to see what he saw, to see reality as it truly was. God answered, and "the LORD opened the eyes of the young man, and he saw" (2 Kings 6:17). What did he see? Myriads and myriads of angels round about Elisha. The heavenly host was there the whole time, but the servant was blinded to that reality. Just like the young servant, we can be blinded. We are blinded by the forces of darkness. This is why Paul says, **Who has bewitched you?** Paul knew the answer; he knew who had bewitched them. It was the only one who had the power to bewitch them to that degree, the power to hide and to conceal and to distort the gospel from the Galatians: Satan.

It was before your eyes that Jesus Christ was publicly portrayed as crucified (v. 1). The language Paul chooses to use here is interesting. John Calvin called for a moratorium on the use of art in worship for at least a temporary period because people during the Middle Ages had begun to give worship to statues. Calvin said, "What the church needs is not more statues but preachers who will so vividly communicate the gospel that when people hear the preaching of the Word of God, it will be so vivid and graphic that it will be as if they are seeing for themselves the very crucifixion of Christ."

Let me ask you only this: Did you receive the Spirit by works of the law or by hearing with faith? (v. 2). This question was significant in the first century. One of the most startling events in the early church was the day of Pentecost when Moses' prayer and Joel's prophecy were fulfilled when God the Holy Spirit empowered the early church and people began to speak in other languages (Acts 2; see Num. 11:29; Joel 2:28). There was not just one such event but four of them.

First, on the initial day of Pentecost, it was the Jews who received the baptism of the Holy Spirit. We read also in the New Testament that those in Cornelius' household who were known as God-fearers received the outpouring of the Holy Spirit (Acts 10), then the Spirit fell upon the Samaritans (Acts 8:4–25), and finally the Spirit fell upon the Ephesians (Acts 19:1–10). Four groups—the Jews, the God-fearers, the Samaritans, and the Gentiles—all received this outward display of the power and anointing of God the Holy Spirit. Now Paul says: "On what basis did you receive the Holy Spirit? Did the Holy Spirit fall upon you Gentiles as a result of your good works? Or was it from the hearing with faith?" It was a rhetorical question. The answer was obvious. The Galatians had done nothing to merit or deserve the outpouring of God the Holy Spirit that they received along with others in the early church.

Are you so foolish? Having begun by the Spirit, are you now being perfected by the flesh? Did you suffer so many things in vain—if indeed it was in vain? Does he who supplies the Spirit to you and works miracles among you do so by works of the law, or by hearing with faith—just as Abraham "believed God, and it was counted to him as righteousness"? (vv. 3–6). This appeal to miracles was an appeal to the certification of agents of revelation. They were enabled by God the Holy Spirit to perform miracles to attest and prove the credentials of the Apostolic community, among whom was included, of course, the Apostle Paul.

Paul is laboring this same point with the Galatians that he labored in his epistle to the Romans: the doctrine of justification by faith alone. In order to prove the doctrine of justification by faith alone, the Apostle Paul didn't claim as his example himself or Barnabas or Timothy or John or Matthew or Mark. Exhibit A for the evidence that justification is by faith alone is Abraham. Just as Paul did in Romans, he now does here in Galatians, pointing to chapter 15 of the book of Genesis where we read that God made a promise to Abraham and Abraham believed God. He didn't just believe *in* God; he trusted God. He believed God, and it was counted to him for righteousness. Abraham was not inherently righteous, but he was counted or considered or regarded righteous because righteousness was given to him or transferred to him by faith, not by works.

Luther struggled with the epistle of James when he was defending the doctrine of justification by faith alone. We read in James 2:21–23: "Was not Abraham our father justified by works when he offered up his son Isaac on the altar? You see that faith was active along with his works, and faith was completed by his works; and the Scripture was fulfilled that says, 'Abraham believed God, and it was counted to him as righteousness'—and he was called a friend of God." "You see," James says, "that a person is justified by works and not by faith alone" (James 2:24). If ever there were a clear, resounding, conclusive, refutation of the doctrine of justification by faith alone, this would be it. You might say, "Well, they're not using the same word for justification; they can't mean the same thing." They're using exactly the same word. James, when he's making his case for justification by works and not by faith alone, uses as his exhibit A the patriarch Abraham.

Paul argues to both the Galatians and to the Romans that Abraham is justified by faith alone. James is arguing that Abraham is justified by works. No wonder the critics of the Bible say the Bible is filled with contradictions. What do we do with this? Luther struggled so much with this verse that he began to wonder about the very canonicity of the book of James, saying, "James is an epistle of straw." Luther later repented of that comment. Paul cites Abraham as evidence of justification by faith alone, citing Genesis 15. When James argues that Abraham is justified by works and not by faith alone, he is citing Genesis 22, which gives us the record of Abraham's offering Isaac as a sacrifice.

Paul is answering one question, and James is answering a different question. Paul's asking, How does a man who is not just, who doesn't have merit in himself, become justified in the sight of God? He answers emphatically and clearly, unambiguously, that it's by faith alone. James is asking a different question. The question James is asking is this: If a man says he has faith and does not have works, will his faith justify him? The answer is no, faith without works is dead. Faith that has a profession but is not manifested by the deeds of obedience is not true saving faith but dead faith. A dead faith never justified anyone. That's why Luther made the statement that justification is by faith alone but not by a faith that is alone.

Paul says that before Abraham did any work of obedience or obeyed any of the laws of God, he was already justified because he trusted God. James is asking, If a man says he has faith but he doesn't have any works to manifest it, will that faith justify him? He says no. He goes on to say that Abraham was justified in Genesis 22 when he offered up Isaac on the altar, proving that the faith that he had was true faith. Before whose eyes was Abraham justified when he offered up Isaac on the altar? He was justified or vindicated when he manifested true faith before human beings. The idea that Paul is getting at is that we cannot know others' hearts. We can know if they have made a profession of faith, but we can't know if their profession is authentic. We have to wait and see the fruits.

How long does God have to wait before He knows whether Abraham's faith is authentic? Did He have to wait seven chapters to see what Abraham was going to do when He commanded Abraham to offer his son Isaac on the altar? The minute God looked at the faith of Abraham, when he trusted in the word of God, God knew with absolute certainty and omniscience that Abraham had saving faith. The very second He saw that, God declared him righteous by faith alone.

Know then that it is those of faith who are the sons of Abraham (v. 7). Again, referring back to Romans, those who are the children of Abraham are not all those who are the descendants of Abraham. Ishmael was a descendant of Abraham, but he was not justified by faith. You are not justified by biology; you're justified by faith. If you call yourself a child of Abraham, the only way you can be Abraham's child is if you share the same faith that Abraham had.

The Scripture, foreseeing that God would justify the Gentiles by faith, preached the gospel beforehand to Abraham, "In you shall all the nations be blessed" (v. 8). Remember that the centerpiece of this epistle is the gospel. The question is, What is the gospel and what is not the gospel? What was under attack among the Galatians was the very gospel of justification by faith alone.

Not only is Abraham an example and an exhibit of justification by faith alone, but Scripture prophetically said that God would justify Gentiles the same way He justified Abraham: by faith. The gospel was preached beforehand to Abraham. Then comes the conclusion: **So then, those who are of faith are blessed along with Abraham, the man of faith** (v. 9).

10

THE CURSE OF THE LAW

Galatians 3:10–14

❦

For all who rely on works of the law are under a curse; for it is written, "Cursed be everyone who does not abide by all things written in the Book of the Law, and do them." Now it is evident that no one is justified before God by the law, for "The righteous shall live by faith." But the law is not of faith, rather "The one who does them shall live by them." Christ redeemed us from the curse of the law by becoming a curse for us—for it is written, "Cursed is everyone who is hanged on a tree"—so that in Christ Jesus the blessing of Abraham might come to the Gentiles, so that we might receive the promised Spirit through faith.

For all who rely on works of the law are under a curse (v. 10). After laboring the point that justification is by faith and not through the works of the law and making it clear "that a person is not justified by works of the law but through faith in Jesus Christ" (Gal. 2:16), Paul now changes the tune just a little bit in terms of the nuance he uses. If you are a student of logic, you will recognize that what the Apostle has written here is a universal affirmative proposition. Also, if you are a student of logic, you may recognize some of the implications of the truth tables by which certain inferences follow from other propositions. Paul is saying that all who do A are also in the state of B.

If you are A, you will also be B. Now, again, Paul is not interested in giving us an abstract expounding of logic, but the logic that he is declaring here is something we dare not miss at the peril of our eternal lives. He says, **All who rely on works of the law are under a curse**. Now, if you are included in that statement **all** and if you have been relying for your justification on obeying the law of God, all you've achieved to this point is to be exposed to the curse of God.

When Paul is speaking to the Judaizers, he certainly has primary reference to the Old Testament law that was given by and through the mediator of the old covenant, Moses. But if we expand the understanding of the law, as Paul does in his epistle to the Romans, we understand that not only the Jews are under the law, but the Gentiles are also under the law. Everyone is under the law of God.

Paul explains in Romans that death reigned from Adam until Moses. The only way that could be is if sin reigned from Adam to Moses. Paul argues in that epistle that where there is no law, there is no sin. God can't hold anybody accountable for sin if He hasn't legislated any behavioral obligations. Since death reigned from Adam to Moses and since death started before the law of Moses was given, the Apostle argues that before the law was published on Mount Sinai, the whole world already knew the foundational precepts of the moral law of God. If you look at the natural law, the *lex naturalis*, or if you look at what's called the *jus gentium*, the law of the nations, you will see that you don't have to have a law written on stone to know that it is wrong to murder. You don't need written documents to know it is wrong to steal another person's property.

We live in a culture that has embraced, as Allan Bloom indicated in his book *The Closing of the American Mind,* the philosophy of relativism. Bloom says that 95 percent of students who graduate from high school and enter college are already convinced of the position of moral relativism, and by the time they graduate from their college experience, that number goes from 95 percent to 98 percent.

It's true that 98 percent will affirm their faith in moral relativism until or unless somebody steals their wallet, and then suddenly, they are marching in protest against some kind of violation or transgression of the moral law of God. We don't need a Bible or a professional ethicist to understand the sanctity of private property or to understand that we are held accountable by the law that God reveals to us not simply on tablets of stone but through the conscience. We are made in the image of God and understand internally the fundamental foundational precepts of what is right and what is wrong. We know that by nature.

For it is written, "Cursed be everyone who does not abide by all things written in the Book of the Law, and do them" (v. 10). All of us are guilty of searing our consciences, of trying to silence the voice of conscience, but even the most callous psychopath or sociopath does not have the ability to extinguish altogether the law of God. We know the difference between what is right and what is wrong, and so we are all under the law. The law stands over and above us, imposing the obligations of our Creator on our behavior. We're under obligation and, in that sense, under the law. What Paul is talking about here, however, is far more serious. He tells us that being under the law involves not only being under obligation to the law but being under the curse of the law.

If there's any word that is foreign to our contemporary vocabulary, it's the word *curse*. Other than using it to describe a certain kind of language, for the most part the concept of cursing has all but disappeared from our culture. Who believes now that curses have the power to actually change a person's destiny? Paul believed it and God believed it.

If we want to understand the significance of the curse, we should go back to the Old Testament, specifically to the book of Deuteronomy. Chapter 28 describes the terms or sanctions of the covenant that God made with Israel in the law of Moses. These sanctions were twofold, both positive and negative. God set before the people the option of blessing on the one hand or curse on the other hand. We read words like this:

> "If you faithfully obey the voice of the LORD your God, being careful to do all his commandments . . . the LORD your God will set you high above all the nations of the earth. And all these blessings shall come upon you and overtake you, if you obey the voice of the LORD your God. Blessed shall you be in the city, and blessed shall you be in the field. Blessed shall be the fruit of your womb and the fruit of your ground and the fruit of your cattle, the increase of your herds and the young of your flock. Blessed shall be your basket and your kneading bowl. Blessed shall you be when you come in, and blessed shall you be when you go out." (Deut. 28:1–6)

Then in stark contrast, the word of God comes to the people of Israel and says: "But if you will not obey the voice of the LORD your God or be careful to do all his commandments . . . then all these curses shall come upon you and overtake you. Cursed shall you be in the city, and cursed shall you be in the field. Cursed shall be your basket and your kneading bowl. . . . Cursed shall you be when you come in, and cursed shall you be when you go out" (Deut. 28:15–19).

To understand these dual sanctions of blessing and curse, we must first understand what blessing is. Many churches use the classic Aaronic blessing at the end of their services every Sunday: "The LORD bless you and keep you;

the LORD make his face to shine upon you and be gracious to you; the LORD lift up his countenance upon you and give you peace" (Num. 6:24–26). The blessing here is communicated through a literary pattern called parallelism, of which there are various kinds. In this case, we have synonymous parallelism, where the same thing is pronounced in three different ways. The three stanzas, as it were, are repetitive. What it means to be blessed as a human being is to be able to have God draw near, lift up His face to you, lift up the light of His countenance upon you. Jesus in the Sermon on the Mount says the pure in heart shall see God. The reason we don't see God is not that He's invisible to us or because we have some kind of impairment in our eyesight; the problem is with our hearts. Because of sin, God hides His face from us. The ultimate blessing that we have awaiting us in heaven is to experience the *visio Dei*, the beatific vision of God wherein we see Him as He is. In the meantime, He remains hidden in part to us.

The curse is the absolute contrast to the blessing. If we were to state what is meant by the curse of God in the Old Testament, it would go something like this: "May the Lord curse you and abandon you. May the Lord turn His face away from you and give you only His judgment. May the Lord turn out the light of His countenance and give you nothing but distress and turmoil." It's the worst of all possible experiences that a human being could endure, to have God turn His back on you, to reject you now and forevermore.

That's why churches end worship services not with the negative warning of judgment but with the positive promise of redeeming grace. We who have placed our trust in Christ look not for condemnation but for redemption, that we might behold Him as He is. Paul starts this section by saying, **All who rely on works of the law are under a curse** (v. 10). Paul has already said that if anybody preaches any other gospel than the one that they had received, that person was to be anathema, cursed. Paul said that if you have heard the gospel and embraced the gospel, if you now turn away from it, the only thing left for you is not the blessing of the covenant but the curse of divine wrath.

For it is written, "Cursed be everyone who does not abide by all things written in the Book of the Law, and do them" (v. 10). I know that people don't believe in the wrath of God. Anytime there's a national crisis, bumper stickers appear announcing, "God bless America," but nobody believes that God would damn America. You can't have a God who blesses who also does not refuse to bless. Paul is now saying that if you're under the law of God—and everybody is by nature—you're under the curse. If you don't put your trust in Christ's righteousness, then you face the curse alone. Paul doesn't think this is a secondary or tertiary issue, a minor point of theology. Rather, it's *the* issue.

Now it is evident that no one is justified before God by the law, for "The righteous shall live by faith." But the law is not of faith, rather "The one who does them shall live by them" (vv. 11–12). Paul goes on to the most succinct expression of the gospel you'll find anywhere in the Scriptures, and perhaps the most poignant: **Christ redeemed us from the curse of the law** (v. 13). Suppose I were to ask you, What is salvation? What does it mean to be justified? How would you answer those questions? The answer is found in the word *redemption*. To redeem is to purchase something, to buy it back.

The theme of redemption runs through Scripture. There were slaves who once were bound but who then were purchased, freed, and liberated, and this provided a picture of the salvation that believers enjoy in Christ. Paul says, "Here's the gospel: you were under the curse of the law, but Christ has redeemed you from the curse of the law." How did Christ do that?

When I hear somebody say that all religions are the same, even if I don't know anything else about him, I realize he doesn't know anything about theology. I know that if he thought seriously about it, he would never make such a statement. If a person spends a short time studying world religions, he will see radical differences among them. Among all religions, though, Christianity is unique. The uniqueness of Christianity is this: it is the only faith that has an atonement.

The difference is Jesus—who Jesus is and what He did. Muhammad did not provide an atonement for guilt. Moses did not free anyone from the curse of the law. Buddha was impotent when it came to freeing a person from the consequences of his sin. In addition, Muhammad is dead; Moses is dead; Buddha is dead. Only One has been vindicated by resurrection.

The way that Jesus redeemed us from the curse was by becoming a curse for us. It wasn't simply that Jesus was cursed in our place, which He was. He took the full measure, penalty, and consequences of disobedience to the law of God on Himself. He who was free from all sins lived a life of perfect righteousness. Jesus had imputed to Him the sin of His people and came under the curse of God. He is the only One who has ever taken on others' sin. Some preachers speak of how painful the cross was with the spikes, the beatings, and the crown of thorns, but I wonder if Jesus even felt those things. He called from the cross in agony, "My God, my God, why have you forsaken me?" (Matt. 27:46). What does it mean to be forsaken by God, to be cursed?

The Father turned His back on Jesus because in the attribution of our sin to Him, Jesus was the most obscene individual in all of human history, so filthy that God couldn't even look at Him. Not only did Jesus receive the curse, but Paul says He became **a curse for us** (v. 13). He was the curse. That's why the Apostle says: "You're not your own. You are bought with a price. You've been purchased by the One who became a curse."

"Cursed is everyone who is hanged on a tree"—so that in Christ Jesus the blessing of Abraham might come to the Gentiles, so that we might receive the promised Spirit through faith (vv. 13–14). Those are the only options we have: the blessing of God and the curse of God. As long as we live by ourselves under the law, we have nothing but the curse of God. That's why Paul pleads with the Galatians to understand that Christ has taken that curse and that they may live not by works but by faith.

11

THE COVENANT

Galatians 3:15–20

To give a human example, brothers: even with a man-made covenant, no one annuls it or adds to it once it has been ratified. Now the promises were made to Abraham and to his offspring. It does not say, "And to offsprings," referring to many, but referring to one, "And to your offspring," who is Christ. This is what I mean: the law, which came 430 years afterward, does not annul a covenant previously ratified by God, so as to make the promise void. For if the inheritance comes by the law, it no longer comes by promise; but God gave it to Abraham by a promise.

Why then the law? It was added because of transgressions, until the offspring should come to whom the promise had been made, and it was put in place through angels by an intermediary. Now an intermediary implies more than one, but God is one.

Earlier in this epistle, Paul makes a statement that he also makes in his epistle to the Romans, that "by works of the law no one will be justified" (Gal. 2:16). He goes on to say that all who are under the law are under the curse of the law. Then he reminds us that Christ, in securing our redemption, became a curse for us, taking upon Himself the curse that God pronounced on all who fail to keep the commandments that were mediated by Moses.

This discussion focuses on covenants. The core pattern by which God brings redemption to pass for His people throughout history is through the structure of covenant. We read about different kinds of covenants that were given in the

Old Testament: the covenant of creation, the covenant with Noah, the covenant with Abraham, the covenant of Moses at Mount Sinai, the covenant with David for the promise of his everlasting kingdom. We read all these passages with respect to the covenant in the Old Testament.

Then in the New Testament, Jesus announces a new covenant that is made in His blood for the remission of sins. In creation, God entered into a covenant with the representative of all of humanity, Adam. We call it the Adamic covenant or the covenant of works.

In classic Reformed theology, a distinction is made between the covenant of works and the covenant of grace. The initial covenant that God made with Adam was based on works. Adam was called to obey the commandments of God. He was placed on probation, and if he kept the law, he would receive the blessing of the Tree of Life. If he broke the law and ate of the Tree of Knowledge of Good and Evil, he would fall under the curse of disobedience. We call that the covenant of works because that covenant was determined on the basis of the performance of human obedience: keep the law of God and you live; disobey the law of God and you die.

We make the distinction between the covenant of works and the covenant of grace even though we understand that God is not obligated to make any covenant with us in the first place. The first covenant He made with Adam was a gracious condescension on God's part. We still make this useful distinction between the covenant of works and the covenant of grace because any redemption that is experienced after the fall of Adam is by the grace of God alone.

Paul labors the doctrine of justification by faith alone to the Galatians in the same way he does in the epistle to the Romans. The Judaizing heretics were trying to bring the believers in Galatia back under the law, saying it's nice to have faith and it's good to trust in Christ, but to be fully saved, we have to go back and fulfill all the terms of the law of Moses. This is the error that Paul addresses when he speaks to the Galatians. Paul reasons that if you have to go back under the law to be justified, you have annulled the perfect work of redemption that has been wrought for us by Christ.

When we say the gospel is that we are justified by faith alone, that is shorthand for saying that we are justified by Christ alone. Ironically, that we are justified by Christ alone also means that ultimately the only way any of us will be saved is by works. Every human being in this world, every creature, is under the covenant of works, and the only way anybody will ever be redeemed is by works.

That's why we have this great contrast established in the New Testament between the work of Adam, whose work was one of disobedience resulting in death's entrance into the world, and the work of the second Adam, Jesus, who keeps the original covenant of works for us. We're saved by works. The issue, however, is whose works? It's not your works or my works but the works of Jesus, the new Adam who fulfills the covenant obligations that were first given to the entire human race. Everybody is in a covenant relationship with God, but by nature we are covenant breakers, not covenant keepers. The whole unconverted world remains under the curse of God for violating the covenant of works. We later see God enter into a covenant with Abraham. This covenant with Abraham is in bold and vivid contrast here in Galatians to the covenant that God makes through Moses at Sinai.

To give a human example, brothers: even with a man-made covenant, no one annuls it or adds to it once it has been ratified (v. 15). Paul is saying that he will give an illustration about covenants in human terms. When a covenant has been made and ratified, it can't be annulled later. Paul is arguing from the lesser to the greater. If this is true with people on a human level, how much truer is it when the covenant is made by God? The covenant God made with Abraham was a covenant not based on works or on merit but based exclusively on God's promise.

People sometimes talk about their life verse, a verse of the Bible that's supposed to be particularly meaningful to them. I'm not sure where this idea came from, since each verse of the Bible is supposed to be our life verse. But when I'm asked what my life verse is, I say Genesis 15:17. People might wonder why I would choose that particular verse. In Genesis 15, God makes a covenant with Abraham, Abraham believes God, and it is counted to him as righteousness. Abraham staggers a little bit at the immensity of the promise and says, "How can I know for sure that these promises will come to pass?"

God instructs Abraham to cut some animals in half and to line up the pieces in two rows. God then puts Abraham to sleep, and Abraham has a vision wherein he sees a flaming or burning pot moving between the animal pieces.

This verse introduces us to a theophany. The fire pot that is moving between the pieces represents God, who is saying: "Abraham, because you want to know for sure that I will keep My promise to you, I'm going to pass between the animal pieces. By doing that, I'm saying to you that if I fail to keep My promise, I will be cut in half, just like these animals that you see. I'm swearing by Myself. What I'm saying, Abraham, is if I don't keep My word, may My immutability become mutated, My immortality become mortal, My eternality become temporal, My omnipotence become impotence, My omniscience become ignorance."

Now the promises were made to Abraham and to his offspring. It does not say, "And to offsprings," referring to many, but referring to one, "And to your offspring," who is Christ (v. 16). As the author of Hebrews tells us,

God could swear by nothing greater, so he swore by himself" (Heb. 6:13). That's the meaning of that text in Genesis, and this is what the Apostle is reminding the Galatians. Notice the use of the term **offspring** is not used of the seed collectively, but Paul says that this offspring refers to **one, . . . who is Christ**.

It harks back again to the early chapters of Genesis where after Adam and Eve commit sin, their eyes are opened and they realize that they are naked and ashamed. God curses the serpent who seduced them, and He says in that curse one of the greatest messages that we hear anywhere in Scripture. It is called the *protoeuangelion* or first gospel, and it tells us that the seed of the woman (singular offspring), though His heel will be bruised, will crush the head of the serpent (Satan). All the way back in Genesis, this verse is looking down the ages to the cross, to the promise of our redemption that comes in the form of a curse on the serpent.

We see the first act of redemption in which God is involved when He sees the nakedness of Adam and Eve and their shame. He makes coverings from animal skins and tenderly condescends to cover their nakedness to hide their shame. In that act of God is the first taste of the glory that is ours in the redemptive work of Jesus, who provides the ultimate covering for sins for His people. With this comes the promise to Abraham and to his offspring, who Paul tells us is Christ.

This is what I mean: the law, which came 430 years afterward, does not annul a covenant previously ratified by God, so as to make the promise void. For if the inheritance comes by the law, it no longer comes by promise; but God gave it to Abraham by a promise (vv. 17–18). The law of Moses was given **430 years** after the promise to Abraham. Paul says the law **does not annul** the promise. Why does God make a covenant with Abraham and later make another covenant through Moses?

In the covenant that was made through Moses at Mount Sinai, there were blessings and there were sanctions. The blessings say that if you keep the law, blessed are you in the country, blessed are you in the city, blessed are you when you sit down, blessed are you when you stand up, blessed are you everywhere. The sanctions say that if you break the covenant and don't keep all the laws that are given in this covenant, then cursed shall you be in the country, cursed shall you be in the city, cursed shall you be when you stand up, cursed shall you be when you sit down, cursed are you everywhere. That's why Paul said earlier in chapter 3 that all who are under the law are under the curse, referring to the standards and the stipulations that are provided in the covenant given through Moses. Which is it? Did acceptance by God come by works of the law or by the grace of the promise? Did God change His mind after He made the promise to Abraham and swore by Himself that He would keep His word? Did God reconsider, saying, "No, wait a minute; I have a plan B. This isn't going to work, so I'm going to give Moses the Ten Commandments and attach blessings and curses"?

Which covenant are we under? One is strictly a covenant of promise; there's no merit, no law, no nothing. The second one is dependent on obedience or disobedience. Paul both asks and answers the question for us here in Galatians. He asks, **Why then the law?** (v. 19). Isn't that the question? If we have a covenant that God unilaterally gives by promise that is by faith, why the law? He answers his own question.

It [the law] **was added because of transgressions, until the offspring should come to whom the promise had been made, and it was put in place through angels by an intermediary** (v. 19). Were there no transgressions before the law? Paul teaches us in Romans that death ruled from Adam to Moses and the punishment for breaking the law is death. Yet there was death in the world long before Moses. Before God gave His commandments on the tablets of stone, people died every day. Paul labors the point in Romans that the law was already written on the human heart, that through nature, God has revealed Himself and His righteousness to every human being and it's being witnessed to by the conscience.

We know that the conscience is not stable, that the conscience can be changed. It can be seared. We can have calluses. We can, as Jeremiah said, have the forehead of the harlot incapable of blushing because we are so accustomed to sinning. But no matter how calloused the worst sociopath or psychopath is, no human being has the power to completely extinguish the conscience. We all know, to at least some degree, the difference between right and wrong. We don't need tablets of stone to know that it is wrong for us to murder somebody. We know that it's wrong to steal. The *jus gentium*, the law of the nations, universally attests to that. It's the law of nature.

Why then the law? Paul provides the answer: **Because of transgressions**. Weren't there always transgressions? Of course there were, but the Apostle is saying that it's not that the law of Moses replaces the promise to Abraham but that it quickens the promise to Abraham. It is as if the descendants of Abraham fell asleep in their consciences. They excused themselves by repeated sins. They deceived themselves into thinking that they didn't need a redeemer who would justify them by faith. When the law was given, it was an enormous wake-up call to everyone in Israel. They read the terms of the law.

We study, read, recite, and memorize the Ten Commandments, not because we believe that if we keep the Ten Commandments we're going to be saved but to help us remember that the just shall live by faith. Every time I look at the law, I look in the mirror and I don't like what I see. The law reveals not only the perfect character of God but also the imperfect character of Sproul. I can't miss the contrast. I can't deceive myself into thinking that I can work my way into heaven. I will never be able to do that. That's why Paul says, "By works of the law no one will be justified" (Gal. 2:16). It's only by the gracious promise of God that is fulfilled in the one offspring, in Christ, that we can be saved.

It was put in place through angels by an intermediary. Now an intermediary implies more than one, but God is one (vv. 19–20). There weren't any mediators with respect to the promise that God made to Abraham. It was direct, unequivocal, and immediate when God spoke to Abraham and promised him salvation. Abraham believed God and was justified. That's the message of the New Testament. That's the message not just of Romans and Galatians but of the whole Bible from Genesis through Revelation. The message is that the righteous shall live by faith. Now, it's not that the law is worthless. Paul will expand on this later and tell us what value the law is, but the primary value initially is to wake us up from our dogmatic slumbers, from our self-deceit, and to make it clear that our only hope is in the abiding promise of God.

12

LAW AND GOSPEL

Galatians 3:21–26

Is the law then contrary to the promises of God? Certainly not! For if a law had been given that could give life, then righteousness would indeed be by the law. But the Scripture imprisoned everything under sin, so that the promise by faith in Jesus Christ might be given to those who believe.

Now before faith came, we were held captive under the law, imprisoned until the coming faith would be revealed. So then, the law was our guardian until Christ came, in order that we might be justified by faith. But now that faith has come, we are no longer under a guardian, for in Christ Jesus you are all sons of God, through faith.

I pointed out earlier that in Galatians 3 we face a difficult problem regarding the difference between the covenant that God made with Abraham, which is a covenant of promise, and the covenant that God made with Moses. The question that was put before the Galatians by the Apostle was this: What's the difference between these covenants, the covenant of Abraham and the covenant of Moses? Did God change His mind in the middle of redemptive history and, instead of redeeming His people solely on the basis of trust and faith in His promise, go in a different direction and decide to base redemption upon obedience to the law?

As Paul contemplated that possibility, his response was no, God made no mistake with the promise that He made to Abraham, and He didn't change His mind. There was no plan B regarding the law given by Moses. Paul asks,

Why then the law? Why did Moses add the prescriptions that God ordained? He answers that question when he says that the law was given because of sin. The point was not that people didn't have any concept of law before Moses; the law was already written on everyone's hearts. By nature, mankind has a basic understanding of right and wrong. The law of God that was implanted in our souls was written on the tablets of stone by the fingers of God so that there would be no mistake about the difference between righteousness and unrighteousness, between obedience and disobedience.

Is the law then contrary to the promises of God? Certainly not! For if a law had been given that could give life, then righteousness would indeed be by the law (v. 21). Paul continues with a discussion on the question of the relationship of the covenant made with Abraham and the law that was given through Moses. Again, Paul asks, **Is the law then contrary to the promises of God?** In the most emphatic Hebrew mode that he could, he answers his own rhetorical question: **Certainly not!** (which is to say "God forbid!" or "By no means!").

Paul has just said that the law was given because of transgressions and that the law revealed that the whole world was imprisoned under the bondage of sin. When Martin Luther and John Calvin reflected on this passage and those related to it, there was a significant difference in their understanding of the purpose of the giving of the law even though they agreed on almost every other significant point of systematic theology. Luther emphasized what he called the *usus elenchticus*—that is, the teaching principle of the law, the law as a schoolmaster that drives us to Jesus. Luther claimed that this is the primary purpose of the giving of the law. Calvin certainly agreed with that principle, but Calvin unfolded three main purposes for the law; the third use of the law is what brought him into conflict with Luther. Let's take a look at these three uses or purposes of the law.

Calvin talked about the law's serving as a mirror, but it is like a double mirror, a mirror that reflects from both sides. On the one hand, the mirror reflects the character of God. On the other hand, the mirror reflects our own character.

Years ago, we had a consultant at Ligonier who asked me this: "What's the single most important thing that you, as a theologian, want to teach people who are not Christians? What do you want to communicate?" I said: "I want to communicate to unbelievers who God is. Unbelievers know *that* God is. God has revealed Himself manifestly to every one of His creatures. Though they might not acknowledge it, everyone knows *that* He is. What they don't know is *who* He is."

The consultant went on to ask, "What's the most important thing you want to teach Christians?" I said: "That's easy. I want to be able to teach Christians who God is because it's the same problem we have with the pagan." Our understanding of the being and character of God is so thin, so superficial, that we, even in our most sanctified state, have almost no understanding of who God is in His majesty and in His being. We don't really understand who we are until we first understand who God is. Once we understand who God is, and we see in that mirror the revelation of God's perfect holy character, we instantly see in that same mirror the radical difference between who God is and who we are.

I've been asked, "What are the important things to remember when you're praying?" There are two things you must remember when you're praying: first, who God is, and then who you are. We don't go into the presence of God and make demands. God is not a cosmic bellhop who exists for our pleasure. When we come into the presence of God, we're on our faces; we're on our knees. That's the only posture we can have in the presence of God because, even though we're justified in Christ, God is holy and we are not. The first point of the law is to reveal who God is and, by contrast, who we are, to make clear that the whole world is imprisoned under the law.

Now before faith came, we were held captive under the law, imprisoned until the coming faith would be revealed. So then, the law was our guardian until Christ came, in order that we might be justified by faith (vv. 23–24). We see that we are in chains when we look at the law of God, and we come to realize that we are helpless to free ourselves from those chains. Paul goes on and speaks here of the law as a **guardian**. Other translations render this word as "tutor" or "pedagogue." The Greek word used here describes a disciplinarian who is hired to govern children who are unruly or incorrigible. Usually, those people who functioned as guardians were brought into the employ of the family to keep the children in line.

Sometimes the word is used to describe a tutor or a schoolmaster in the classroom, but when we think of a schoolmaster, what image comes to mind? The most common is that of the person who is standing up in the front of the class giving instruction. That's what we hire our teachers to do. However, that's not the figure that is used here in Galatians. Here, the person in view is responsible for discipline in the classroom.

Perhaps you've seen pictures of old classrooms with the teacher in front of the blackboard and another person walking the aisles while carrying a long pole. That pole was in the hands of the schoolmaster. He was watching for any students who were nodding off or daydreaming. The schoolmaster would rap them on their knuckles to make them pay attention. If they began to be restless and squirmed in their seats or were caught chewing gum or any such offense, the schoolmaster would apply harsh discipline.

Think of Pharaoh, who imprisoned the people of Israel and governed them harshly. He required that they make so many bricks, and if they failed to produce the right number, they felt the lash. To make it harder, he withdrew the ration of straw that was given to help make the bricks, and the Hebrew people were then compelled to make bricks without straw. The Bible talks about Pharaoh as a harsh taskmaster who ruled by the sweat of the brow of his people. That's what the law is and what the law does. The law comes and crushes us. As soon as we look at the law, we know that we are lawless. We try to excuse ourselves. We try to give rationalizations for our misbehavior, but we don't have to dig very deeply into our souls to know that we have not obeyed the law of God.

Think of the rich young ruler who Jesus met in Luke 18. He came to Jesus, saying, "What must I do to inherit eternal life?" (v. 18). Jesus responded, "You know the commandments: 'Do not commit adultery, Do not murder, Do not steal, Do not bear false witness, Honor your father and mother'" (v. 20). The rich man responded, "All these I have kept from my youth" (v. 21). He conveyed an attitude of complacency: "Is that all? I've obeyed every one of the Ten Commandments from the time I was a little boy, so it will be easy for me to enter the kingdom of God." Jesus didn't argue with the young man but just pointed to the first commandment: "You shall have no other gods before me." Jesus told the rich young ruler to sell everything he had and give it to the poor, and then he could follow Him.

The man walked away sorrowful, for he had many possessions. This fellow, so hardened in his own heart, actually believed that he had kept the law from his youth. Clearly he was absent when Jesus gave the Sermon on the Mount, wherein Jesus explained the real demands of the law. Had the rich young ruler been there, it would have been clear to him that he hadn't kept even one of the Ten Commandments for one minute of his life.

That's what Luther learned in the monastery. That's why he spent many hours in confession every day. Luther reflected on the great commandment found in Matthew 22:37–39: "You shall love the Lord your God with all your heart and with all your soul and with all your mind. . . . You shall love your neighbor as yourself." Luther thought that since that's the great commandment, then the great transgression must be to fail to love the Lord your God with all your heart, with all your mind, and with all your strength. These kinds of thought kept Luther's confessors busy. In any case, the schoolmaster, the guardian, kept people imprisoned. That was what the law did, but that was just the first function of the law.

The second function of the law that Calvin articulates is to exercise restraint on people, to act as a bridle. Part of God's common grace is to keep us from being as evil as we actually are in our hearts. One of the great distinctions the forefathers or founders of this country made was between the rule of people and the rule of law. We are not a democracy. We were never intended to be a democracy. Democracy is ruled by people—majority rules. There's no Bill of Rights governing a democracy; it's mob rule. We're a republic, which means we are governed by the rule of law. No one is above the law.

Looking at all the laws passed over the course of American history, one might wonder why people ever say that you can't legislate morality. If this means that the business of Congress is never to spend time legislating morality, then they don't have much left to do. They can determine the national flag or the national bird or something like that, but when you establish speed limits on the highway or you establish laws against theft, laws against murder, laws against child molesting, these are all moral issues. What is meant by the phrase "You can't legislate morality" is that you can't change the behavior of people just by passing a law.

In fact, many times the Scriptures tell us that the more laws we pass, the more people are incited to sin. So what's the point of having laws when we break them all the time? Calvin was stating this idea: "Imagine if there were no laws at all, how reckless we would be on the highway, how dangerous we would be to people around us. If there were no restraints, it would be anarchy, the law of the jungle, the law of total violence. In this situation, might makes right." One of the gracious reasons that the law was given is not only to teach us our hopeless and helpless condition but to restrain us from being as bad as we could possibly be.

When it comes to the third use of the law, Calvin gave one of his greatest contributions. He talked about the revelatory function of the law, that the law reveals what is pleasing to God. If you're a Christian, it isn't because you kept the law. You're a Christian by grace. You're justified by faith, not by works. So now that the law has done its work and has driven you to Christ and you're justified and sanctified, what good is the law?

Jesus put it this way: "If you love me, you will keep my commandments" (John 14:15). He was saying in effect, "Don't tell Me you love Me and then obstinately refuse to obey Me." The heart of a Christian is to say this: "Lord, what would You have me do? I ask not so that I can earn my way into heaven, for I know that's an impossibility. And besides, my reservation is already assured there. I know I can't work my way there. But because I'm Yours, I am working to do everything I can to please You."

The psalmist says in Psalm 119:97, "Oh how I love your law!" What's strange about this text is not only that somebody who is a child of God would say that they love the law, but I think the most important word in this segment of the psalm is the first word. The psalmist doesn't simply say, "How I love Your law." Rather, he begins with "Oh," which is an expression of passion, of profound feeling. It's not some secondary affection for the law but pure delight. It's the kind of delight spoken of in Psalm 1, which says of the righteous man, "His delight is in the law of the LORD, and on his law he meditates day and night" (v. 2).

The Christian world is filled with antinomians. They declare that once they have become Christians, the law has nothing more to say to them. However, the law reveals what is pleasing to God.

> Oh how I love your law! It is my meditation all the day. Your commandment makes me wiser than my enemies, for it is ever with me. I have more understanding than all my teachers, for your testimonies are my meditation. I understand more than the aged, for I keep your precepts. I hold back my feet from every evil way, in order to keep your word. I do not turn aside from your rules, for you have taught me. How sweet are your words to my taste, sweeter than honey to my mouth! Through your precepts I get understanding; therefore I hate every false way. (Ps. 119:97–104)

Finally, the psalmist says in verse 105, "Your word"—or we could substitute "Your law"—"is a lamp to my feet and a light to my path." We don't have to grope and fumble around in darkness with our feet slipping off the path and falling into distractions, for God has given us the light of His law to reveal what things please Him.

But now that faith has come, we are no longer under a guardian, for in Christ Jesus you are all sons of God, through faith (vv. 25–26). The law is powerless to save us, but it serves its functions in driving us to Christ, restraining sin, and revealing what pleases God. The law pointed forward to our need for a Savior, and that Savior has now arrived in the person of Christ Jesus. Now the law shines that much more in the lives of God's adopted children to show us where we should walk lest we fall into destruction.

13

IN CHRIST

Galatians 3:27–29

For as many of you as were baptized into Christ have put on Christ. There is neither Jew nor Greek, there is neither slave nor free, there is no male and female, for you are all one in Christ Jesus. And if you are Christ's, then you are Abraham's offspring, heirs according to promise.

For as many of you as were baptized into Christ have put on Christ. **There is neither Jew nor Greek, there is neither slave nor free, there is no male and female, for you are all one in Christ Jesus** (vv. 27–28). This text has been the center of enormous controversy, and much mischief has been done with respect to this passage. The focal point of the controversy centers on the Apostle's teaching elsewhere related to the calling of wives to be in submission to their husbands.

To address these matters, we must acknowledge that we have seen great changes in our day. Cultural changes over the past few decades have led some to call into question these passages on wives' relationships with their husbands. It is thus said in some circles that the Apostles Paul and Peter were misogynists because they taught that wives should be in submission to their husbands. The thought is often: "How could you teach that unless you hated women?" That's the conclusion that some come to. Of course, that creates a slur not only on Paul and Peter but also on the One who appointed them and gave them their Apostolic authority—namely, the Lord Jesus Christ.

A few weeks ago, we had dinner with some friends who had formerly been missionaries in Russia, and they told us that they had gone back to visit the church they had established there. They brought pictures back to show to my wife and me. The thing that struck me when I looked at the pictures of this church body was that every woman in the church was wearing a hair covering. I said, "They must've missed the cultural revolution that we went through in the United States."

The photos made me think back to the various customs we've followed in America. One of my memories from when I was a child in the forties and in the fifties is being in the boys' church choirs. We had to wear a certain uniform to sing in the choir. It consisted of a black cassock covered by a shorter surplice, and we had a stiff white collar around our neck with a giant black bow. I hated to go outside on the way to church because if any of my friends saw me, they would laugh and say, "Look at little Lord Fauntleroy going to church to sing." Later on, I also sang in the junior high choir and then the senior high choir with the adults in the chancel choir. My church, which was a very large church in that day, was a progressive church. Every girl in the junior and senior high choir had to wear a little beanie attached to her head with hairpins or bobby pins. Every woman in the chancel choir wore the same kind of head covering without exception. On Sunday morning, every woman in the congregation came to church wearing a hat.

As I looked at my friend's pictures of the congregation in Russia, I thought about the customs that they are still observing in Russia and what my own background had been. All my experiences had taken place before the cultural revolution of the sixties. Since the cultural revolution, which was couched in phrases of liberation theology, there has been much mischief. At the heart of this liberation theology was liberation that involved gender-neutral behavior, same-sex marriage, abortion, and even attacks on the sacred institution of marriage. Many young people are now choosing not to be married but rather to live together without the benefit of the sacred vows of marriage. How much has the church been influenced by this revolution in the culture?

In 1 Corinthians 11, Paul gives the instructions that women should cover their heads in worship. This is a difficult passage to understand. Commentaries give a variety of different views on it. Some commentators say that the reason that the Apostle called women to cover their heads is that their glory is in their hair, and they ought to cover that glory when they come to church in the presence of God and the angels. Many commentators look at this passage and say, "This is clearly based on what was a contemporary custom of the culture in Corinth, and so Paul is just repeating that customary practice from the first century." I've always been disturbed by that explanation because Paul doesn't appeal to local custom in the text.

Instead, Paul appeals to creation, saying that this is the order that God established in creation—that is, the woman was created out of the man and not the man out of the woman (1 Cor. 11:8–9). One of the most difficult portions of the text is when he speaks about the hair covering as a symbol that is "because of the angels" (1 Cor. 11:10). What does that mean? At church on Sunday morning, do you think about whether you wear a hat because there may be angels there? What does he mean by "because of the angels"? There have been numerous interpretations of that, some of them quite strange. There are common issues in the epistle to the Hebrews and Paul's letter to the Galatians. One of the main concerns of the author of Hebrews is to tell the reader what happens in corporate worship, where we are and why we are in worship.

Hebrews tells us, "Let us consider how to stir up one another to love and good works, not neglecting to meet together, as is the habit of some, but encouraging one another, and all the more as you see the Day drawing near" (Heb. 10:24–25). When we come to our worship service, we come into the presence of God. We come into the presence of Christ. We come into the presence of angels and archangels and the fellowship of "the righteous made perfect" (Heb. 12:23), the commonwealth of heaven. Our worship experience involves the communion of saints, and we're not in isolation from other Christians around the world. We are bound by our spiritual unity in Christ with the whole church—the whole church now, the whole church of the past, and the church that exists in heaven. When the author of Hebrews talks about how we are to conduct ourselves in church, he's aware of the heavenly aspect, the sacred aspect of worship; he's aware that we're coming in submission to our Lord.

Obviously, the church has to relate to whatever culture in which it finds itself. One of the things I was taught in seminary from the higher critic professors is that the original documents of Scripture are culturally bound, that everything in the Bible reflects the culture of the times in which the Bible was written. If we want to learn anything from the Scriptures that would have any application for today, we have to cut through all that was binding people in the ancient world. In seminary, we learned the Hebrew and Greek languages, studying the words and grammar in order to interpret the Bible. The other thing we had to do was to study what we called the *Sitz im Leben*, which is from the German language meaning the life situation in which the Bible was written. Then we had to consider which principles or ideas we find in Scripture that carry over to future generations. How much of Scripture was written because of the prevailing culture of the time?

Some of these issues are fairly simple. When Jesus gave His instructions to the seventy-two whom He sent out to proclaim the kingdom of God, He told them not to wear shoes (see Luke 10:4). We can't extrapolate from that episode that there's a divine principle that the only legitimate form of evangelism must be done in bare feet. When we pay our tithes, we don't pay with denarii and drachmas. Different forms of currency move in different countries; clothing patterns differ in different countries. Those are all kinds of things that we know are creations of particular cultures and customs. Is the Bible simply a matter of culture?

Some say that we can't take the Bible literally, that it is simply a series of moral pronouncements cloaked in allegory. There are certainly allegories in the Bible, but genre analysis reveals that the Bible contains a variety of literary forms. There are historical narratives, poetic structures, and many others. We have to differentiate among the different literary forms we encounter if we're going to understand the Bible, but thankfully the various genres themselves tell us how they should be understood. We understand this intuitively when we read other works of literature—we read poetry as poetry and fiction as fiction. This points to an important principle, which is that we read the Bible as we read any other book. In the Bible, a verb is a verb and a noun is a noun; there's no such thing as Holy Ghost Hebrew or Holy Ghost Greek that changes the rules of grammar and historical interpretation.

Going back to the business about women's hats, I do not think that the question of head coverings is the article upon which the church stands or falls, but I also don't think it's insignificant. We're supposed to be faithful in the small things as well as in the large things. The question is what is dictating our behavior. The whole business of culture has two sides to the coin. We look back and we are removed two thousand years from the New Testament and four thousand from the Old Testament. We're historically removed from all these teachings, and we're trying to understand the Word of God, which rules forever. We know that we aren't living in the first century. We're living in the twenty-first century, so we're not familiar with every custom that was founded in the first century or previous centuries.

We're always trying to figure out what the life situation was when the Bible was written, and that's important. Even more important than how the culture influenced the writing of the Bible is how our culture now influences us in our understanding of the Bible. I suspect it's not the Bible but the influence of our contemporary culture that influences our ideas about the sanctity of marriage, the sanctity of life, gender neutrality, and other related concerns. We are not to be conformed to the contemporary standards of this world. The Apostle Paul tells us not to be conformed to this world but to be transformed, rising above the standards and the customs of our own day to seek the mind of Christ. We are to ask ourselves not what the latest fashion or custom is in our culture but what honors Christ. That should be the primary question.

I have a chapter in my book *Knowing Scripture* on trying to discern the difference between a custom, which is bound to a time and place and culture, and a principle, which has enduring authority and significance. In that chapter, I use the text in 1 Corinthians 11 as the illustration of the problem. Suppose you don't know, and you can't figure it out. Then what? The Bible gives us some direction about it. If it's not in faith, it's sin (see Rom. 14:23). Therefore, if I don't know what the text requires, whether it is a custom or it is a principle, I need to walk in faith. If I treat it as a principle when it was actually a custom, I am going to be guilty of being overly scrupulous and maybe even legalistic. If it's a principle and I dismiss it as a custom, now I'm in defiance of God.

It may be best to walk on the safe side. Don't bring upon yourself the displeasure of your Savior. Study the Bible, read 1 Corinthians 11, and see what you understand God to be saying in that passage. I leave it to you, to your conscience, and to the Word of God, and I ask that in all these things, we may glorify Him.

Finally, what is the basic point of Galatians 3:27–29? When the Apostle says there's **neither Jew nor Greek**, he's not denying that there are ethnic differences between a Jew and a Greek. He goes into great lengths, for example, in Romans 11 to talk about the distinction between the Jews and the Gentiles. All throughout the New Testament, that distinction remains. Likewise, though Paul says **there is neither slave nor free**, he gives specific instructions for how to deal with slaves in the book of Philemon. He doesn't say that there's no difference between masters and slaves. There's a serious and significant difference. And though he says **there is no male and female**, he is not saying that there is no difference between males and females.

What Paul is saying is simple. Being a Jew, being a Gentile, being a woman, being a man, being free, being a slave—no matter what, the ground is level at the foot of the cross. Nobody has any advantage in the kingdom of God because they're a man or because they're a woman. Nobody has an advantage in the kingdom of God because they're a Gentile or because they're a Jew. Nobody has anything of which to boast if they are master or if they are slave. We are **all one in Christ Jesus**. In Christ, we are united with the same dignity and the same sweetness of our situation and status in the kingdom of God. That's what Paul is saying, and he's rebuking the Galatians for wanting to make the difference permanent between Gentile and Jew, so that the Gentiles would be considered second-class Christians. In the kingdom of God, there's no such thing as a second-class Christian, for **if you are Christ's, then you are Abraham's offspring, heirs according to promise** (v. 29).

Again, it doesn't mean that the distinctions between Jew and Gentile, slave and free, male and female, are obliterated. Of course that's not what Paul is talking about. He's talking about our standing at the foot of the cross. That's where everything is level, and that's a glorious thing for us to understand.

14

ADOPTED HEIRS

Galatians 4:1–7

I mean that the heir, as long as he is a child, is no different from a slave, though he is the owner of everything, but he is under guardians and managers until the date set by his father. In the same way we also, when we were children, were enslaved to the elementary principles of the world. But when the fullness of time had come, God sent forth his Son, born of woman, born under the law, to redeem those who were under the law, so that we might receive adoption as sons. And because you are sons, God has sent the Spirit of his Son into our hearts, crying, "Abba! Father!" So you are no longer a slave, but a son, and if a son, then an heir through God.

Our contemporary church and culture are far less influenced by the heritage of the Reformation than by the great revolution of the eighteenth and nineteenth centuries. Though the movement of the Enlightenment was not monolithic, the central thesis of the Enlightenment was that mankind no longer needed to depend on the idea of God to explain the universe or human life. The great discovery was that spontaneous generation had produced the origin of the universe and of human life. Such thinking is philosophical and theological nonsense, but it captured the minds of so many in the eighteenth century.

What happened broadly across Europe but particularly in Germany in the nineteenth century was even worse: theological liberalism. Nineteenth-century theological liberalism essentially succumbed to philosophical theories of naturalism.

In theological liberalism, we saw the denial of the virgin birth, the resurrection of Christ, the atoning death of Christ, the authority and inspiration of the Bible, and the miracles of Jesus, among other things. Historic and classical Christianity was stripped of all its essential truths and was replaced by a new humanitarian religion called theological liberalism.

One of the great crises that theologians faced in the nineteenth century was this: What do we do with the church? They understood that the church for nineteen hundred years had rested its whole reason for existence on the biblical principles of the incarnation of Christ, the resurrection of Christ, the atoning death of Christ, and so on. Once these things were abandoned, what function was left for the church? Some came to the conclusion that there was no function left for the church and that it should be discarded. Others said the church is an ongoing institution that has great influence in terms of humanitarian principles, so it should be continued.

Another key question was this: What's the unique contribution of Christianity to world religion? There were some who said there is no unique contribution but that all religions at their root are basically the same. The theologian and historian Adolf von Harnack wrote a book in which he tried to extrapolate the essence of Christianity. He concluded that the unique foundational truths of the Christian faith are the universal fatherhood of God and the universal brotherhood of man. The irony is that neither one of these concepts is taught in the Bible.

The Bible doesn't teach the universal fatherhood of God, though there is a vague quote from a pagan poet to this effect (Acts 17:28). Paul acknowledged that we are all God's offspring in the sense that we are all God's creatures; we were all created by God.

Every time the Scriptures talk about the fatherhood of God, the concept in view is not something universal but something gloriously particular. It does not apply to everybody, and it only applies to one person by nature—namely, Jesus Christ, who is the *monogenēs*, the only begotten of the Father. Ultimately, the only Son of God is Jesus. We are able, as Paul points out in this passage, to participate gloriously in the family of God, not naturally but supernaturally—that is, by adoption.

If you're a child of God, it's because He has adopted you, not because you were born one. This is the argument that Jesus had with the Pharisees when they claimed to be the children of Abraham. Jesus said, "No, you are of your father, the devil" (see John 8:44). The Scriptures teach us that we are by nature the children of wrath. Yet our culture keeps repeating this nineteenth-century lie that we're all the children of God. We're not. We are by nature children of Satan.

What about the universal brotherhood of man? What the Bible teaches is the universal *neighborhood* of man. All of us are neighbors. That's why we are called universally to love our neighbors as ourselves. If my neighbor is not a Christian, if my neighbor is a pagan, if my neighbor hates the gospel, I'm still required to love my neighbor. We're all in this together as neighbors. But the brotherhood is special. Those who participate in the brotherhood are those who are part of the family of God, and only those who participate in the family of God by adoption are part of the brotherhood.

One of the tools we have to help us in our understanding of the New Testament is a study of the Bible's *Sitz im Leben*, the life situation out of which the Bible arises. Far more important, however, is the understanding of our own culture and how much it influences our understanding of the Word of God. In countless ways, our contemporary culture blinds us to the plain teachings of the Word of God. Looking at the church today and at what it was in the sixteenth century or in the first century, we see that the contrast is overwhelming. Today, the church is a daughter of the revolution of the nineteenth century. I'm not talking only about the mainline churches that have no basic beliefs at all. I'm talking about evangelical churches that are overwhelmingly influenced by the trends of our society and by the trends of our culture. We derive our ethics from what's happening in the world around us rather than from the Word of God. We're Christians. We're citizens of the commonwealth of heaven. It's the Word of God that is to be the foundation of our truth and our faith and our beliefs.

John Calvin commented on Galatians 4:1 and raised this question: Why would somebody divide this book into chapters and separate chapters 3 and 4, ripping apart the connection between the two chapters? When Paul wrote his letter, he didn't write, "Dear Galatians, chapter 1, verse 1." Then a bit later write, "Chapter 2." No, he wrote a letter. There weren't any verses. There weren't any chapters. There was coherent unity of the word that the Apostle taught. Calvin was concerned about the division at chapter 4 because the ideas of chapter 4 are so related to what Paul had already said, that in Christ, there's neither Jew nor Greek, neither slave nor free, neither male nor female, for believers are all one in Christ Jesus. If you are Christ's, then you are Abraham's and heirs according to the promise. He is introducing this concept of a legacy that the people of God enjoy, that we are in the Father's will, not the will of purpose or design, but His last will and testament, the last will and testament that was announced by our Savior before He died. He said: "Peace I leave with you; my peace I give to you. Not as the world gives do I give to you" (John 14:27). Jesus was speaking about an inheritance, a bequeathment of peace, because we are heirs of God and joint-heirs with Christ.

I mean that the heir, as long as he is a child, is no different from a slave, though he is the owner of everything, but he is under guardians and managers until the date set by his father (vv. 1–2). If you are an heir or an heiress, you are in a sense no different from anybody else until you receive your inheritance. Before you receive your inheritance, you are under a guardian, a tutor. Paul has already talked about all of us, but particularly the Jews, being under a tutor—the Old Testament law. As long as the law was functioning as a guardian and tutor over the people of God, they were not free. They had not experienced the fullness of their inheritance. When somebody is an heir, his inheritance is set off in the distance while he's still a child until some point in the future when he is old enough to receive it. During childhood, he's no different from a slave. Even though he's the owner of everything, he's still like a slave under guardians and managers until the day set by his father for him to come into his inheritance.

When somebody has a will, or the patriarchs had blessings to give, no one would receive the benefits of the will or the blessing until the day that was appointed by the father. Some of you may be involved in trust funds. The trust funds say you come into your trust at age twenty-five or age fifty or when your parents die, but there's a day that is established by law when the inheritance now becomes yours. In the meantime, you may have a future promise, but you don't possess the inheritance.

In the same way we also, when we were children, were enslaved to the elementary principles of the world (v. 3). Now there's some debate about what Paul means about the **elementary principles**. Is he saying that when you were children, you were under the influence of astrology and the principles that are associated with all kinds of idolatry? Perhaps. Maybe he's talking to us in the contemporary sense that when you were a child, you were under the influence of every pagan idea that came along. That could be said of us, unfortunately, even after we were children.

When the fullness of time had come, God sent forth his Son (v. 4). Paul speaks of a concept that we hear elsewhere in the Scriptures where he speaks of the *plērōma*, the fullness of time. To understand what *plērōma* means and the concept of the fullness of time, I like to use the illustration of a glass of water that is three-quarters of the way filled. That's not *plērōma*. Even if you fill the glass to the edge of the lip, it's still not *plērōma*. *Plērōma* happens when you put the glass under the faucet and the water fills up the glass and starts running over the sides of the glass because there's no space left to contain it. God had appointed a time—not just the year or the week or the day, not even just the hour or the minute, but the very second. From all eternity, God said, "In that precise second, the virgin will give birth to My Son." That was the day the glass was filled to overflowing by the providence of God. The birth of Jesus into this world was not an accident. It was according to God's divine purpose, down to the very second.

In Acts 17:30–31, Paul says, "The times of ignorance God overlooked, but now he commands all people everywhere to repent, because he has fixed a day on which he will judge the world in righteousness by a man whom he has appointed; and of this he has given assurance to all by raising him from the dead." The Scriptures tell us that it's appointed to man to die once, and after that comes the judgment (see Heb. 9:27). We will stand in the presence of Almighty God and all the fullness of His majesty and power and holiness. If we are not clothed in the righteousness of Christ, we will never escape that judgment. So many of us don't believe there will be a judgment. We like to think that God is so loving that He tolerates anything. "Do what you want." That's the ethic of our culture. People's ears are stopped up and they don't hear the word of the promise, that God will judge the world on that appointed day.

But here, Paul isn't talking about judgment. He talks about the **fullness of time** when **God sent forth his Son, born of woman, born under the law** (v. 4). Jesus didn't just come down from heaven in a parachute on Good Friday and go to the cross to save us from our sins. For Him to be the Redeemer, He had to first fulfill **the law.**

We think of the resurrection of Christ as a singular and unique event, and in a sense it is, but other people have been raised from the dead. The one thing that is absolutely unique in all human history is the sinless life. Without that sinless life, we have no redemption. But Jesus lived a sinless life, obeying the law in every dimension on our behalf.

. . . to redeem those who were under the law, so that we might receive adoption as sons (v. 5). If you believe in the universal fatherhood of God, it will not be surprising to hear us called sons of God. Harnack, after all, said we're all children of God. But Jesus said we are children of the devil. Jesus had a better understanding than Adolf von Harnack did of who is included in the family of God. To be called **sons** of God is an incredible privilege, and those who proclaim the universal fatherhood of God miss this privilege.

And because you are sons, God has sent the Spirit of his Son into our hearts, crying, "Abba! Father!" (v. 6). No one can properly pray to the Lord and say "Our Father" or open prayer with the words **"Abba! Father!"** who has not been born of the Spirit of God. Only those who are born of the Spirit are given by the Spirit the right to presume to call God "Father." It's been said by one New Testament scholar that in every prayer of Jesus recorded in the New Testament, He addresses God as Father in all but one. Yet when we pray "Our Father" as Jesus told us to, we think, "What's so important about that?" It is radical that Jesus said we now have the privilege, the filial right, to address God as Father through the power of the Holy Spirit.

So you are no longer a slave, but a son, and if a son, then an heir through God (v. 7). Paul tells the Galatians that if they understand what it means to be a Christian, they won't go back to slavery. They won't return to bondage and worry about whether to keep new moons and sabbaths and whether to get circumcised. He says that the law is a tutor, a guardian until you receive the inheritance. The fullness of time has come, and Christ has come, so you don't have to wait for your inheritance anymore. You've been adopted into the family of Almighty God and given the unspeakable privilege of saying, "Abba, Father."

15

DAYS AND SEASONS

Galatians 4:8–20

Formerly, when you did not know God, you were enslaved to those that by nature are not gods. But now that you have come to know God, or rather to be known by God, how can you turn back again to the weak and worthless elementary principles of the world, whose slaves you want to be once more? You observe days and months and seasons and years! I am afraid I may have labored over you in vain.

Brothers, I entreat you, become as I am, for I also have become as you are. You did me no wrong. You know it was because of a bodily ailment that I preached the gospel to you at first, and though my condition was a trial to you, you did not scorn or despise me, but received me as an angel of God, as Christ Jesus. What then has become of your blessedness? For I testify to you that, if possible, you would have gouged out your eyes and given them to me. Have I then become your enemy by telling you the truth? They make much of you, but for no good purpose. They want to shut you out, that you may make much of them. It is always good to be made much of for a good purpose, and not only when I am present with you, my little children, for whom I am again in the anguish of childbirth until Christ is formed in you! I wish I could be present with you now and change my tone, for I am perplexed about you.

Formerly, when you did not know God, you were enslaved to those that by nature are not gods. But now that you have come to know God, or rather to be known by God, how can you turn back again to the weak and worthless elementary principles of the world, whose slaves

you want to be once more? (vv. 8–9). Paul begins this section by giving us two distinct contrasts––between freedom and bondage and between knowing God and not knowing God. The two are inseparably related. If you don't know God in a saving way, you're in bondage. You may think that you're free and enjoy vast liberties in your life, but ultimately, if you don't know God in a saving way, you're in chains.

Paul's second contrast says, "You did not know God and instead you gave service and obeisance to those things that are not God, to those things that are actually idols. You served and worshiped things that were made by your own hands, things that are creatures, and all the while you did not know God." That's perplexing because Paul begins his letter to the Romans in this way: "For the wrath of God is revealed from heaven against all ungodliness and unrighteousness of men, who by their unrighteousness suppress the truth. For what can be known about God is plain to them, because God has shown it to them. For his invisible attributes, namely, his eternal power and divine nature, have been clearly perceived, ever since the creation of the world, in the things that have been made. So they are without excuse" (Rom. 1:18–20).

The "ungodliness and unrighteousness of men" is summed up in suppressing the truth—that which God has revealed about Himself plainly and manifestly to every person in the world through the things that are made. God's self-revelation is so clear that "they are without excuse."

What excuse will people want to use on the day of judgment when they stand before God? "O God, I was agnostic; I didn't know that You were there. If only I had known that You exist, if only I had known that You reign over heaven and earth, my life would have been different. I would have been Your servant; I would have been obedient." Paul says that excuse will be ruled out of order. The last excuse anybody will be able to give is ignorance.

Paul goes on to say:

For although they knew God, they did not honor him as God or give thanks to him, but they became futile in their thinking, and their foolish hearts were darkened. Claiming to be wise, they became fools, and exchanged the glory of the immortal God for images resembling mortal man and birds and animals and creeping things.

Therefore God gave them up in the lusts of their hearts to impurity, to the dishonoring of their bodies among themselves, because they exchanged the truth about God for a lie and worshiped and served the creature rather than the Creator, who is blessed forever! Amen. (Rom. 1:21–25)

Paul emphasizes that every single person knows God, and the basis for our judgment is that we do know Him.

People deny God everywhere in the world. I once was invited to an atheist club at a university where I was asked to defend the existence of God. Before I started, I said: "Let me put my cards on the table. I'm perfectly willing to stand before you and give what I believe is incontrovertible proof of the existence of God, but I realize that in so doing, I'm in a sense wasting my time because I am convinced that you already know that God exists, and you know it clearly. You know it not only through the things that are made, through the creation, but also internally, with the conscience that you can't quiet. You know that God is. The problem is not that you don't know God; your problem is that you hate Him, that you want to get Him out of your mind and get Him out of your lives because you have reprobate minds." I didn't make a whole lot of friends that night. They weren't happy about what I said, but Paul makes it abundantly clear that no one has an excuse because everybody already knows that God exists.

Yet, here in Galatians Paul speaks of not knowing God. Does Paul contradict himself? Not at all. In 1 Corinthians 1:21, he says that they did not know God according to human wisdom. When Paul talks about the knowledge of God, he uses a word that's important in the New Testament. It's the Greek word *gnōsis*, meaning "knowledge."

Knowledge as a biblical concept has two different references. On the one hand, it refers to a cognitive awareness. Every creature in the universe has an intellectual or cognitive awareness of God. At the same time, this word has a much deeper meaning, describing personal intimacy. When the Bible says that Adam *knew* his wife and she conceived, it isn't saying that Adam had a cognitive awareness of Eve's identity and therefore she got pregnant. The word *to know* is used for the deepest knowledge of intimacy.

This is the concept that is in view in Galatians 4. Paul says, "You didn't know God in that sense, but now you know God." However, Paul then clarifies what he means: **You have come to know God, or rather to be known by God**. What's the difference? Isn't it the same thing to know God as it is to be known *by* God? Again, there are two different ways you can talk about being known by God.

Some people believe that from all eternity, the foreknowledge of God precedes His predestining of His saints to salvation. Isn't it true that God knows everybody in the world, even before they're born? Yes, He knows them cognitively—but He doesn't know them savingly. If He knew them savingly, then every creature would be saved, but it is a special, distinct blessedness to be known by God in a salvific way.

In the Sermon on the Mount, Jesus delivers a severe warning: "On that day many will say to me, 'Lord, Lord, did we not prophesy in your name, and cast out demons in your name, and do many mighty works in your name?' And then will I declare to them, 'I never knew you; depart from me, you workers of lawlessness'" (Matt. 7:22–23). In the final analysis, it's not whether you know Jesus that matters; it's whether Jesus knows you. He knows all about you, but does He know you in a saving way? Did He from time eternal choose you in the Beloved and know you in Christ?

How can you turn back again to the weak and worthless elementary principles of the world, whose slaves you want to be once more? You observe days and months and seasons and years! (vv. 9–10). What's he referring to? He's not referring to the natural distinctions of days and weeks and years that are determined by the rotation of the planets and by the sun. He's talking about days that have been set aside, months and seasons that have been set apart in redemptive history, including such things as the Jewish feasts, the Day of Atonement, the Feast of Weeks, and the year of Jubilee.

He says that these were **elementary principles**; these were things that God gave to His people to observe in the past. They were the shadows of things that were to come. Yes, it was obligatory for every Jew in the Old Testament to celebrate the Passover and Yom Kippur and so on, but Paul explains that if you insist on celebrating these days after the advent of Christ, you have missed the whole gospel. The whole point of the Day of Atonement, for instance, was to point ahead to the ultimate sacrifice and the blood of the Messiah that would be offered once and for all, never again to be repeated. After that finished work of Jesus was accomplished, it would be foolish to go back to the shadows, to the prefigurements, for we are no longer under that obligation.

When God establishes a law, does it last forever? No, it doesn't. We distinguish in theology between God's natural law and God's purposive law. Be careful that you don't misunderstand what I'm saying because we have another way of speaking of natural law. We talk about the *lex naturalis*, the law of nature that is revealed in nature and conscience, and the *jus gentium*, the law of the nations, where there's a universal agreement among all peoples that certain things are right and certain things are wrong.

By the law of God's nature, there are certain laws that God reveals and legislates based on His own nature, His own character. His nature and His character are immutable; they never change in the slightest. There's a second set of laws that God gives in history known as the purposive laws of God—namely, the particular items of legislation for a specific, defined, historical purpose. When that purpose is finished and fulfilled, that law is abrogated. We no longer celebrate Yom Kippur; we celebrate the Lord's Supper. We don't celebrate the Passover or the Feast of Weeks or any of those.

But God doesn't change the prohibition against idolatry when He says, "You shall have no other gods before me." Now that the new covenant has come and we're not under the bondage of law, may we serve and worship idols? No. If God allowed idolatry, it would be for Him to deny Himself, to deny His character, and to deny His very being. So, God's natural law never changes.

Here, Paul's talking about the historical, purposive laws of the Old Testament that governed the days and the times and the seasons. He says that's all gone. Paul implores them, **Brothers, I entreat you, become as I am** (v. 12). He's saying that he is not subject to the old economy anymore. He does not observe those days and seasons. He is a Jew, a Pharisee of Pharisees, but he does not observe those things anymore because they have been fulfilled. He is not in bondage to them anymore, for he is free in Christ.

You did me no wrong. You know it was because of a bodily ailment that I preached the gospel to you at first (vv. 12–13). The phrase **bodily ailment** has attracted a great deal of scholarly interest. Scholars want to dig in and find out what this bodily ailment was. At another time, Paul talked about having a thorn in the flesh, and he also spoke about writing with big letters, possibly because his vision was impaired (2 Cor. 12:7; Gal. 6:11).

Maybe he was saying that he had poor eyesight and people could see him groping around as if he could barely make out the movement of people; maybe that's how they had to deal with him mercifully. Others have argued that he suffered from epilepsy. I don't really know what Paul's physical infirmity was.

In 2 Corinthians 11:21–29, Paul gives a quick autobiography:

But whatever anyone else dares to boast of—I am speaking as a fool—I also dare to boast of that. Are they Hebrews? So am I. Are they Israelites? So am I. Are they offspring of Abraham? So am I. Are they servants of Christ? I am a better one—I am talking like a madman—with far greater labors, far more imprisonments, with countless beatings, and often near death. Five times I received at the hands of the Jews the forty lashes less one. Three times I was beaten with rods. Once I was stoned. Three times I was shipwrecked; a night and a day I was adrift at sea; on frequent journeys, in danger from rivers, danger from robbers, danger from my own people, danger from Gentiles, danger in the city, danger in the wilderness, danger at sea, danger from false brothers; in toil and hardship, through many a sleepless night, in hunger and thirst, often without food, in cold and exposure. And, apart from other things, there is the daily pressure on me of my anxiety for all the churches. Who is weak, and I am not weak? Who is made to fall, and I am not indignant?

Paul's body must have been one mass of scar tissue. I don't think he walked boldly into the Galatians' presence; he limped, massive scars all over his body. Most people would look at this figure, at how grotesque he appeared, and would shy away from him in embarrassment. Paul said they didn't do that; they didn't do him any wrong when he preached the gospel to them at first.

And though my condition was a trial to you, you did not scorn or despise me, but received me as an angel of God, as Christ Jesus. What then has become of your blessedness? For I testify to you that, if possible, you would have gouged out your eyes and given them to me. Have I then become your enemy by telling you the truth? (vv. 14–16). There is no quicker way to make enemies than to tell people the truth.

They make much of you, but for no good purpose. They want to shut you out, that you may make much of them. It is always good to be made much of for a good purpose, and not only when I am present with you, my little children, for whom I am again in the anguish of childbirth until Christ is formed in you! (vv. 17–19). He's talking about the false teachers in Galatia. But this time, he doesn't call the Galatians foolish or bewitched. Instead, his pastoral heart begins to come out, as he calls the Galatians **my little children** and says he is **in the anguish of childbirth** about them.

Isaiah 53 gives us a graphic description of Christ, the suffering Savior. We read of the stripes and the lashes and the beating and the humiliation that our Savior had to endure. Isaiah says in verse 8, "As for his generation, who considered that he was cut off out of the land of the living, stricken for the transgression of my people?" He never married or had children. And yet, the Bible talks about the pangs of our Savior's suffering and compared those pangs to the travail of childbirth, the pain that Jesus had to endure for His redeemed children.

Paul now speaks in that same language, the language of childbirth. He says: "I went through anguish to bear you in the first place; now I'm going through that travail all over again until Christ is formed in you. You've begun in Christ, you're born in Christ, but now you need to grow up in Christ that Christ may be formed in you."

This message is for us. The whole point of our sanctification is that Christ may be formed in us. It's not something that Paul was teaching to the Galatians that's different from what he would preach to us. He would say, "You're reading my epistle two thousand years after I wrote it, but where are your heads? Where are your hearts? You've been known by God. What are you doing? Why are you moving away from the gospel?" We all do it.

We can't just say, "We have been redeemed by the travail and the birth pangs of Christ Himself. Does Christ have to go through that again that we may grow up to maturity in Him that He may be formed in us?" That's what He wants, the formation of His people, that He Himself may be formed in you and in me. That's what the Christian faith is about. It's not just about conversion and then you're done. Conversion is the beginning of the Christian life, and then we have our whole lives in which He is making and molding us, shaping and forming us in His image.

I wish I could be present with you now and change my tone, for I am perplexed about you (v. 20). Paul acknowledges that his tone is such that the Galatians might be perturbed by it. But he's not angry—he's hurt; he's devastated; he's confused. He longs for in-person fellowship with the Galatians, for then he could express his care for them and speak in loving tones of peace and comfort. Likewise, thanks to our redemption in Christ, the Lord Himself speaks to us not in anger but in tenderness because we are His.

16

HAGAR AND SARAH

Galatians 4:21–31

Tell me, you who desire to be under the law, do you not listen to the law? For it is written that Abraham had two sons, one by a slave woman and one by a free woman. But the son of the slave was born according to the flesh, while the son of the free woman was born through promise. Now this may be interpreted allegorically: these women are two covenants. One is from Mount Sinai, bearing children for slavery; she is Hagar. Now Hagar is Mount Sinai in Arabia; she corresponds to the present Jerusalem, for she is in slavery with her children. But the Jerusalem above is free, and she is our mother. For it is written,

> "Rejoice, O barren one who does not bear;
>> break forth and cry aloud, you who are not in labor!
> For the children of the desolate one will be more
>> than those of the one who has a husband."

Now you, brothers, like Isaac, are children of promise. But just as at that time he who was born according to the flesh persecuted him who was born according to the Spirit, so also it is now. But what does the Scripture say? "Cast out the slave woman and her son, for the son of the slave woman shall not inherit with the son of the free woman." So, brothers, we are not children of the slave but of the free woman.

I t was the night of my twenty-fourth birthday. I was going back to our apartment after working at a basketball court in the East Liberty section of Pittsburgh. As I walked past a jewelry store, a man ran out with a woman behind him screaming, "Stop, thief!" The jewelry store had just been robbed, and the thief ran out the door and right into me. Reflexively, not out of any sense of heroism, I grabbed the thief and said, "Hold it right there." He looked at me and said, "I give up."

I held him for a few minutes until the police arrived. They took him into custody, and I continued back home for my birthday dinner. A few days later I saw one of the policemen who had made the arrest. I asked, "What happened to that fellow?" He replied, "The man had just been released from jail on the day of the robbery. He had spent so much time in jail previously that it had become his comfort zone." The robber liked being in jail. He had a roof over his head and three meals a day, so when he was released and had his freedom, he didn't want that freedom. To make sure he was returned to incarceration, he robbed the jewelry store, and I was the one who helped him achieve what he was seeking.

Can you imagine anybody who gets out of jail who can't wait to go back? That's what Paul is saying to the Galatians. **Tell me, you who desire to be under the law, do you not listen to the law?** (v. 21). Paul pleads: "Do you not hear what the law is saying? I've labored the point with you that the law is a tutor and a guardian to lead you to the gospel. When the gospel came, you embraced it, but as soon as you embraced it you wanted to go back to the law. It's as though you want to go back to jail."

For it is written that Abraham had two sons, one by a slave woman and one by a free woman. But the son of the slave was born according to the flesh, while the son of the free woman was born through promise (vv. 22–23). Abraham had **two sons**, Ishmael and Isaac. God had promised Abraham in his old age, when his wife, Sarah, was beyond the years of childbearing, that Abraham would have a son and would be the father of a great nation. This was the basis of the Abrahamic covenant. Though he likely expected the promise to be realized imminently, Abraham had to wait and wait as he grew older and his wife remained barren. Finally, at the urging of Sarah, Abraham produced a son with Sarah's slave, Hagar, and the child was named Ishmael. God said Ishmael was not the promised son.

Then Sarah became pregnant. She gave birth to a son, and he was named Isaac. He was born of a **free woman**, and he was **born through promise**.

Now this may be interpreted allegorically (v. 24). The Apostle Paul explains that there's more significance to this story than the mere history of it. Now, we must be careful. This doesn't give us a license to find allegories throughout Scripture. Paul had the authority to understand the allegorical significance of the Old Testament passage, but we don't have that kind of authority. This is just a personal word of caution.

These women are two covenants. One is from Mount Sinai, bearing children for slavery; she is Hagar. Now Hagar is Mount Sinai in Arabia; she corresponds to the present Jerusalem, for she is in slavery with her children (vv. 24–25). It's a long way from **Mount Sinai** to Jerusalem, but Paul says that present Jerusalem is still under the law. The present Jerusalem is still in bondage. The present Jerusalem is like Mount Sinai in Arabia. She still thinks that she can be redeemed by and through the law, and she doesn't know that she is **in slavery**.

The Bible has a lot to say about freedom and slavery. I often hear protests against Reformed theology because many people don't like to hear about the sovereignty of God. They insist, "We have free will." I reply, "Yes, we have free will, but remember Augustine and his debate with Pelagius." Augustine said we have free will, or *liberum arbitrium*, the power and the ability to choose freely what we want. However, at the same time, we are also in slavery. We are in bondage to sin.

Most people who think about free will today think of it in terms of a humanistic, pagan understanding. They understand free will as the equal power of indifference to choose good or to choose evil, that we have the same ability and power to obey God as we have to disobey God. That perspective refuses to acknowledge the reality of Adam's fall, which was catastrophic for the whole human race.

Pelagius argued that Adam's sin affected only Adam and nobody else. The Bible says that Adam's sin affected everybody else: you, me, the whole human race (Christ excepted). The entire human race was plunged into corruption, into moral slavery. Augustine said the faculty of choosing is still there. I'm still able to think, to add two and two and come up with four, but at the same time, my mind has been seriously impaired by sin. My mind is filled with darkness. I don't want to have God in my thinking in my natural state. Likewise, I still have the faculty of choosing. I have a will, and I can always choose what I want to choose. The problem is with the "want to." We don't *want* God. We don't want to choose God. In a sense, the irony is that our freedom is at the same time bound in slavery because our hearts are corrupt and our inclinations are "only evil continually" (Gen. 6:5).

We can still choose, but the only choice we have is to say no to God. Augustine said we still have free will; what we don't have is *libertas*, liberty, the moral ability to choose God, because we are not inclined to choose God. To be free means to choose according to your inclinations. I've heard critics of this say that God is sovereign, of course, but His sovereignty is always limited by human freedom. If God's sovereignty is limited by human freedom, then who is sovereign? Man is sovereign. No, we have freedom, but our freedom is limited by God's sovereignty. We're free, but God is more free.

I've heard people say that God saves every person He possibly can, but that God's power to save is limited by our freedom; God can't save anybody who doesn't first want to be saved. They go on to say that the Holy Spirit is a gentleman, and He would never impose His will on us, forcing somebody against his will to come to faith.

Imagine Paul traveling to Damascus with letters of authority to continue persecuting Christians. Suddenly, as he travels, a stranger appears to him, saying, "Excuse me, may I please have a word with you?" Paul responds: "Yes, of course. What do you have in mind?" The stranger replies, "I would like to suggest that you may be doing the wrong thing, and perhaps you should return to Jerusalem and repent of this evil idea of persecuting Me." "Persecuting You? Who are You?" Paul scoffs. "I'm Jesus, the One you're persecuting, and I would like to ask you in a gentlemanly way to please stop." That, of course, is not what happened. The Apostle Paul, breathing out fire, had one choice in mind. The one thing he willed to do with all his heart was to crush the church in Damascus.

Jesus Christ said, "Stop right there." God intervened. It's not true that the Holy Spirit is a gentleman. The Holy Spirit is not a gentleman. The Holy Spirit is not any kind of man at all. The Holy Spirit is a sovereign God, and without His intervention in your life and in mine, we would still be in bondage. Paul is saying to the Galatians: "Be done with that bondage. The Spirit has set you free. The gospel has come into your midst. The Holy Ghost has intervened and has brought you to saving faith."

But the Jerusalem above is free, and she is our mother (v. 26). Heaven and the gospel are our mother; just as Sarah gave birth to the children of promise, so heaven has brought us to be children in the family of God.

For it is written, "Rejoice, O barren one who does not bear; break forth and cry aloud, you who are not in labor! For the children of the desolate one will be more than those of the one who has a husband." Now you, brothers, like Isaac, are children of promise. But just as at that time he who was born according to the flesh persecuted him who was born according to the Spirit, so also it is now. But what does the Scripture say? "Cast out the slave woman and her son, for the son of the slave woman shall not inherit with the son of the free woman." So, brothers, we are not children of the slave but of the free woman (vv. 27–31). Paul cites the Old Testament exclamation from Isaiah 54:1. He states that we as Christians are also **children of promise**, and that we will be **persecuted** by the world, those who are born

according to the flesh. This was the case with Isaac and Ishmael, and it is the case for us now. But we can rejoice in the midst of our troubles, for **we are not children of the slave but of the free woman** and therefore recipients of the promises of God.

17

CIRCUMCISION
AND LAW

Galatians 5:1–12

For freedom Christ has set us free; stand firm therefore, and do not submit again to a yoke of slavery.

Look: I, Paul, say to you that if you accept circumcision, Christ will be of no advantage to you. I testify again to every man who accepts circumcision that he is obligated to keep the whole law. You are severed from Christ, you who would be justified by the law; you have fallen away from grace. For through the Spirit, by faith, we ourselves eagerly wait for the hope of righteousness. For in Christ Jesus neither circumcision nor uncircumcision counts for anything, but only faith working through love.

You were running well. Who hindered you from obeying the truth? This persuasion is not from him who calls you. A little leaven leavens the whole lump. I have confidence in the Lord that you will take no other view, and the one who is troubling you will bear the penalty, whoever he is. But if I, brothers, still preach circumcision, why am I still being persecuted? In that case the offense of the cross has been removed. I wish those who unsettle you would emasculate themselves!

One of the most serious controversies of the Protestant Reformation of the sixteenth century had to do with this question: What is the instrumental cause of our justification? The medieval Roman Catholic Church held that the instrumental cause, the means by which justification takes place, is the sacrament of baptism.

The Protestant Reformers said baptism is valuable and an important sign of the new covenant community, but it is not the instrumental cause of justification. It is not the means by which we are justified before God. The Reformers claimed that the sole instrumental cause of our justification is faith. When the Reformers spoke about justification by faith alone, part of what they were saying in the term *alone* was that the only instrument by which we are justified is faith.

For freedom Christ has set us free (v. 1). Paul is not speaking redundantly here. He is using a grammatical construction called the instrumental dative to say that the obvious reason or purpose for which we have been liberated from the curse of the law is **for freedom**. It is Jesus who sets us free.

Stand firm therefore, and do not submit again to a yoke of slavery (v. 1). I can just hear Luther at the Diet of Worms when he was called upon to renounce his teaching of justification by faith alone. He responded: "Unless I am convinced by sacred Scripture or by evident reason, I cannot recant, for my conscience is held captive by the Word of God, and to act against conscience is neither right nor safe. Here I stand."

Luther wasn't standing still; he was standing firm. He was immovable. He refused to compromise. Paul was encouraging a similar attitude in the Galatians: Stop wavering. Stand fast. Hold to the gospel.

In his classic work *Christianity and Liberalism*, J. Gresham Machen wrote that Christians come in different stripes and that there are points and doctrines on which we disagree such as Calvinism versus Arminianism, Apostolic succession versus non-Apostolic succession, and Presbyterianism versus Congregationalism. We can disagree on these points without destroying the Christian faith, but the issue of justification by faith alone is no minor incidental matter. It is the article on which the church stands or falls. The Apostle calls us and the Galatians to **stand firm** and not to submit again to **a yoke of slavery**.

Throughout its history, the church has had to battle heresy on almost every issue, on both sides of the issues. In this case, Paul is dealing with the problem of legalism. Legalism has many different forms, but the primary error of legalism is the idea that by obeying the law you can be saved. The opposite heresy is antinomianism, which literally means "anti-lawism" and what is called libertinism. Today, at least in the life of the church in America, we are seeing an epidemic of antinomianism that says we're not only free from the law in terms of its curse, but we are free from the moral law of God to such a degree that we can sin all we want and still have remission of sin as long as we have made a profession of faith. This pernicious and self-contradictory doctrine of the *carnal Christian* has spread throughout the world. It propounds that a person can be a Christian and remain unchanged by Christ and the work of the gospel.

We have to be careful on both sides neither to embrace legalism nor to embrace antinomianism. Paul is speaking against both antinomianism and legalism here. The **freedom** on which Paul focuses here is not political freedom or rescue from some kind of tyranny, but it's freedom from the yoke of the law, from that bondage under the curse of God's judgment. Why would anybody trade that in?

Look: I, Paul, say to you (v. 2). Paul is speaking as an Apostle of Jesus Christ, with nothing less than the authority of Jesus Christ and on nothing less than the authority of God. He speaks not as one of the people who were troubling the Galatians with false teaching but as the one who started the church in Galatia and therefore has authority over it.

If you accept circumcision, Christ will be of no advantage to you. I testify again to every man who accepts circumcision that he is obligated to keep the whole law. You are severed from Christ, you who would be justified by the law; you have fallen away from grace (vv. 2–4). Paul doesn't despise circumcision. He understands the value and meaning of circumcision in the economy of redemption in the Old Testament.

Abraham was justified by faith. Paul labors the point in Romans that Abraham believed God and it was counted to him for righteousness (Rom. 4). Before Abraham was justified, before he had done any of the works of the law, God justified him, counted him righteous. Then, as a sign of the covenant that God made with Abraham, He commanded Abraham to be circumcised, and not only Abraham, but his seed also. So, for thousands of years, every male child in the Hebrew community underwent circumcision. Circumcision had a double meaning.

It was a dramatic symbol and sign of the covenant where the foreskin of each male child was severed. On the one hand, the positive sign of circumcision was that it was a mark of cutting, indicating that God had cut His people out of all the human races to be His people. God was saying that Israel would be His people, and He would bless all nations through this covenant with Abraham. The sign of that blessing—of being cut out, separated, sanctified, consecrated from all the rest of humanity—is circumcision. The negative sanction of circumcision was that every Hebrew male carried the sign on his body that if he disobeyed the covenant made through Abraham with God, he would be cut off from the glory and from the blessing of God just as his flesh has been cut off from him.

There was the positive sign, the sign of blessing, and the negative sign, the sign of curse. If one believed in the promise, he received the blessing. If he denied the promise, he received the curse. When the significance and meaning of circumcision was fulfilled in Christ, Christ Himself received the negative sign of circumcision. He was cursed on the cross, cut off from the land of living, cut off from all the blessings and the presence of God for us. Christ has received the ultimate circumcision so that we may not feel the weight of the cross or of the curse.

The Judaizers were arguing that a person could not be saved unless he was circumcised. Paul says that the whole meaning and significance of circumcision had been fulfilled. Christ was made the curse for you. He fulfilled the law for you, and now you want to insist on circumcision again? You're putting yourself under the law again with all the consequences that attend to it. Circumcision was a wonderful sign, a glorious sign of what God had promised for the future, but now that future has been fulfilled, and you want to replace the gospel with the old covenant sign? If you do that, you're obligated to keep the whole law, and you have been cut off, you have been **severed from Christ**.

The original point of circumcision was to be severed or cut off *unto* Christ. Now Paul warns of being cut off or severed *from* Christ. **You who would be justified by the law; you have fallen away from grace**. That is to say, you have lost your grip on grace. You've failed to understand what grace is. The Apostle Paul is setting before the Galatians an either/or proposition. Either go back to the law or have the gospel; you can't do both.

If you choose the Judaizing heresy, thinking that you can be justified and saved, that it's a necessary aspect of salvation to keep the ceremonies of the law, you have denied Christ. You have denied His gospel. You can't have it both ways. It's either Christ and His gospel or going back to the law.

For through the Spirit, by faith, we ourselves eagerly wait for the hope of righteousness (v. 5). One of the well-known mottos that Luther used was *simul justus et peccator*, at the same time just and sinner. Rome said you can't have it both ways—you can't be justified unless you truly are just or righteous. You have to be inherently righteous in order to be justified. Luther said no, we are justified by faith, by the imputation of the righteousness of Christ to our account. We're not justified by our own righteousness, by some kind of inherent righteousness in us. We're justified by what Luther called an "alien" righteousness, a righteousness that is *extra nos*, outside of us. That's the glory of the gospel, that God counts me as righteous not because I'm righteous but because Christ is righteous. He is our righteousness.

Rome calls this a legal fiction, saying that the only way God will ever pronounce a person just is if the person is in fact just, not by some transfer or imputation of someone else's righteousness. Paul says that **through the**

Spirit, by faith, we ourselves eagerly wait for the hope of righteousness. What is **hope**? Hope is not having a desire that something will take place but remaining uncertain as to whether it will come to pass. Rather, hope is the anchor for our souls. Hope is faith looking to the future. What the Apostle Paul tells us is that by the Spirit, in faith, we are given not just faith, but we are given the hope and assurance of our ultimate future righteousness. Everyone who has faith this day, today, has the righteousness of Christ. It is a certain hope.

When we die, we will be glorified, and then we will be inherently righteous. When we're in heaven, we won't be *simul justus et peccator*, at the same time just and sinner. There, we will be sinless. There will be no sin at all in our glorification. We will be thoroughly and gloriously righteous, and we hope, with assurance and certainty, for the day this will take place in heaven.

For in Christ Jesus neither circumcision nor uncircumcision counts for anything, but only faith working through love (v. 6). "Aha," the Roman Catholic Church says. "See, faith is not alone. Faith has to be working through love, and so it's really faith *and* love that justify you." No. It's faith alone that justifies you, but if you have true faith, solid faith, it will always manifest itself in and through love. The grounds of our justification is not my love or your love; it's Christ and His righteousness.

You were running well. Who hindered you from obeying the truth? (v. 7). Does he ask who hindered them from obeying the law? No, he says they were hindered from **obeying the truth**. Some Christians say, "Doctrine doesn't matter; truth doesn't matter." The Apostle Paul is calling his people not simply to learn the truth but to understand the truth and to know the truth. Truth is not an abstract conceptual matter biblically; it is life and death. Truth is Christ. As Christ said to Pilate: "For this purpose I have come into the world—to bear witness to the truth. Everyone who is of the truth listens to my voice" (John 18:37). Jesus is essentially saying that those who are His hear His voice and love the truth. However, if someone doesn't love the truth, he will never obey the truth. Truth is set before us, not simply to pass a theological exam but as the rule of life, of obedience to Christ.

This persuasion is not from him who calls you. A little leaven leavens the whole lump. I have confidence in the Lord that you will take no other view, and the one who is troubling you will bear the penalty, whoever he is (vv. 8–10). Having mentioned that someone has been hindering the Galatians, Paul returns to the subject of the false teachers, saying that their teaching is not from the Lord. He calls for an imprecation on them, saying that anyone who is teaching contrary to the gospel **will bear the penalty**.

But if I, brothers, still preach circumcision, why am I still being per-secuted? In that case the offense of the cross has been removed (v. 11). Paul preached the cross, and that was the offense. Then Paul gives one of the weightiest maledictions of his entire ministry: **I wish those who unsettle you would emasculate themselves!** (v. 12). He's not just wishing circumcision on the Judaizers who were troubling the Galatians about circumcision. No, Paul is saying much more than that. He is actually wishing that they would be castrated.

Paul was aware of the pagan religions and those who would work themselves up to a frenzy and actually castrate themselves as a religious rite. Paul says, in effect, "If you want to follow these pagan notions of the Judaizing heresy, then you might as well include with it the rite of castration."

18

WORKS
OF THE FLESH

Galatians 5:13–21

For you were called to freedom, brothers. Only do not use your freedom as an opportunity for the flesh, but through love serve one another. For the whole law is fulfilled in one word: "You shall love your neighbor as yourself." But if you bite and devour one another, watch out that you are not consumed by one another.

But I say, walk by the Spirit, and you will not gratify the desires of the flesh. For the desires of the flesh are against the Spirit, and the desires of the Spirit are against the flesh, for these are opposed to each other, to keep you from doing the things you want to do. But if you are led by the Spirit, you are not under the law. Now the works of the flesh are evident: sexual immorality, impurity, sensuality, idolatry, sorcery, enmity, strife, jealousy, fits of anger, rivalries, dissensions, divisions, envy, drunkenness, orgies, and things like these. I warn you, as I warned you before, that those who do such things will not inherit the kingdom of God.

Some people remember World War I and World War II, followed by the Cold War and Korea, Vietnam, and a host of other hot spots in this world. These wars were dreadfully catastrophic, but they're nothing compared to the warfare of which the Apostle Paul speaks here.

We're talking here not about battles between the Allies and the Axis but rather about the cosmic conflict between the Spirit of God and the flesh of man, two entities that are in sharp antithesis, an ongoing and constant battle. If you sign up for this war, you have signed up for the duration, because the end of this war will not take place until we get to heaven. In the meantime, we are not fighting against flesh and blood but are battling powers and principalities, spiritual wickedness in high places. Our fundamental battle is between God and ourselves.

In this passage, Paul introduces the idea of warfare between the spirit and the flesh. To understand what he is saying, we need to define what he means by *flesh*. It's easy to jump to the conclusion that the flesh refers to the physical nature of our human bodies, but that would be a fatal rush to judgment. That's not what the Apostle is talking about here.

In the Greek New Testament, there are two words that are used to describe the physical nature of humans. There is the word *sōma*, which is the normal word used to describe the physical body. We have the word taken into our English language when we speak of psychosomatic illnesses. Those are illnesses that are of the body, but they originate in the psyche or in the mind.

The other word to describe human bodies is *sarx*. This word can also refer to our physical nature. For example, when Paul said that he never met Christ during His earthly ministry, he said he never met Christ *kata sarka*, "according to the flesh." Paul never saw Him in His bodily incarnation. Christ appeared to Paul later, after His ascension into heaven.

There are occasions when the term *flesh* does refer simply to our physical bodies, but not always. The main use of *flesh* in the New Testament is not with respect to our physical bodies but with respect to our fallen human condition, our corrupt nature. In theological terms, it describes what we call original sin.

Original sin does not describe the first sin that was committed by Adam and Eve. Rather, original sin refers to the result of the first sin committed by Adam and Eve. It signifies God's judgment on the human race, of whom Adam and Eve are representatives. Original sin includes the loss of our original righteousness, the guilt of Adam and Eve's transgression, and the corruption into which we are all born.

When Adam and Eve sinned, their sin did not affect them alone; their sin affected the whole human race. The nature of all humanity was changed by the fall. The normal way that the Apostle speaks about this corrupt and fallen nature of mankind is with the term *flesh*. When we see a contrast expressed in the New Testament between spirit and flesh, the Apostle is talking about the Holy Spirit versus our fallen human nature.

In John 3, we read the story of Nicodemus, a Pharisee who came to visit Jesus at night. Nicodemus said to Jesus, "Rabbi, we know that you are a teacher come from God, for no one can do these signs that you do unless God is with him" (v. 2). Jesus went directly to the point with this theologian and ruler of the Jews. He said, "Truly, truly, I say to you, unless one is born again he cannot see the kingdom of God" (v. 3).

There's so much misunderstanding about what it means to be born again. To use the term *born-again Christian* is like stuttering. That's like saying, "I'm a Christian Christian," because everybody who is born again is a Christian, and anyone who is not born again is not a Christian. All kinds of people profess to be Christians, though, and that's why this distinction has come along. We say, "I don't mean just a Christian in general but a true Christian, one who has been regenerated by God the Holy Spirit."

As Jesus speaks with Nicodemus, He says emphatically to him, "Truly, truly, I say to you, *unless* one is born again he cannot see the kingdom of God" (emphasis added). People sometimes tell me that they believed, and then they were born again. If, however, you're not born again first, you will never come to faith. You can't even see the kingdom of God without the prior work of God the Holy Spirit in changing the disposition of your soul.

Then Nicodemus replies to Jesus, questioning what he thought he just heard: "How can a man be born when he is old? Can he enter a second time into his mother's womb and be born?" (v. 4). Jesus ignores his response and states something similar to His previous statement: "Truly, truly, I say to you, unless one is born of water and the Spirit, he cannot enter the kingdom of God" v. 5). First, Jesus says Nicodemus can't see the kingdom of God, then He says he can't enter it. Why? Now Jesus answers the question that is so relevant to our study of Galatians: "That which is born of the flesh is flesh, and that which is born of the Spirit is spirit. Do not marvel that I said to you, 'You must be born again'" (vv. 6–7). Jesus is saying that if you're not born again, you're in the flesh and only in the flesh.

Jesus also said, "The flesh profiteth nothing" (John 6:63, KJV). Martin Luther commented that "nothing" is not "a little something"; it's "nothing." Unless the Holy Spirit changes the disposition of your soul, you are flesh and nothing but flesh. If you are nothing but the flesh, you will perish and profit nothing.

We've seen many people, under the influence of evangelism, make professions of faith. They make decisions to become Christians, raise their hand in a meeting, sign a pledge card, walk down an aisle, say the sinner's prayer, or use some other technique of making a profession of faith. Many pastors and evangelists are eager to say: "That person made a profession of faith. He counts. He's in the kingdom."

There are millions of people who have made professions of faith who aren't anywhere near the kingdom of God. A profession of faith has never saved anyone. A person who is saved is called to make a profession of faith, but just because you make a profession of faith doesn't mean that you possess the faith you need to be justified.

Jesus said, "This people honor me with their lips, but their heart is far from me" (Matt. 15:8). Lip service never saved anybody. No person is really a Christian if they have made a profession of faith but have not had the Holy Spirit change their constituent nature. Such is not just a theological statement, but it is a manifest impossibility. Anybody who is born of the Spirit of God is a changed person.

Paul talks about our ongoing battle with carnality. Anybody who is a Christian is involved in this warfare every day. However, the term *carnal Christian* describes somebody who is only flesh and does not have the Spirit of God dwelling within him.

I once talked to a young man who claimed to be a Christian. He was using drugs, selling drugs, and living with a girl who was not his wife. I said, "How can you be involved in these things and be a Christian?" He said, "Don't worry; I'm a carnal Christian."

Here's what happens when you are converted. You are now in Christ and so you have the Holy Spirit, but the flesh has not been destroyed. It hangs around and we battle with the flesh from now until the day we enter heaven, where we will be glorified. In the meantime, we still battle the remnants of our fallen nature, our flesh.

For you were called to freedom, brothers. Only do not use your freedom as an opportunity for the flesh, but through love serve one another (v. 13). How do we know where we stand in terms of the kingdom of God? Here Paul gives the answer. Yes, we've been liberated, and with the Spirit of God there is liberty, but at the same time, we cannot live however we want; we cannot indulge our flesh. That is called libertinism. It's one thing to have liberty; it's another thing to be a libertine.

For the whole law is fulfilled in one word: "You shall love your neighbor as yourself." But if you bite and devour one another, watch out that you are not consumed by one another (vv. 14–15). Here Paul begins to describe fleshiness and the danger it poses. The remaining flesh, even among Christians, has the power to violate the second great commandment to love our neighbors as ourselves. When we give freedom to fleshly desires, we begin to **bite and devour one another** like we're wild animals. It's not just nipping at the heels of other people but biting and consuming them.

But I say, walk by the Spirit, and you will not gratify the desires of the flesh (v. 16). Here, **the Spirit** is capitalized, and rightly so in that text because it's a reference to the Holy Spirit. If you've been born of the Spirit and the Spirit of God dwells in you, then you need to **walk** according to the Spirit of God, not gratifying **the desires of the flesh**.

People sometimes say, "Come to Jesus and all your problems will be over." One of the happiest days of my life was the day I came to Jesus. But that was the day my life started to get complicated. Augustine says, "When you're still in the flesh, you have a rider on your back, the devil." In Ephesians, Paul speaks of life before Christ as "following the course of this world, following the prince of the power of the air" (Eph. 2:2). The devil was riding on your back; he had the reins. His bit was in your mouth, and you did what he wanted you to do. When you become a Christian, Satan doesn't jump out of the saddle and run away, but the Holy Spirit is now in the saddle. The Spirit grabs the reins, and Satan does everything he can to rip those reins out of the Spirit's hands and to dominate your life.

If you walk in the Spirit, you're not going to gratify the desires of the flesh. When Paul says **you will not gratify the desires of the flesh**, the first thing we think about is physical, sensual desires. These types of desires are included, no question, but when Paul talks about gratifying the desires of the flesh, he's talking about the desires of the fallen, sinful nature. Those evil desires don't just include the body, but they include the mouth, they include the heart, they include the mind, they include the whole person.

For the desires of the flesh are against the Spirit, and the desires of the Spirit are against the flesh, for these are opposed to each other, to keep you from doing the things you want to do. But if you are led by the Spirit, you are not under the law (vv. 17–18). This struggle is not simple. In our sanctification, we are called to "work out [our] own salvation with fear and trembling, for it is God who works in [us], both to will and to work" (Phil. 2:12–13). But at the same time, this is a cosmic battle. It's a battle for our soul every second.

Now the works of the flesh are evident (v. 19). To say that these **works** are **evident** means that they are not subtle. They're not so mysterious that you have to search to find out what the **works of the flesh** are. They're manifest. Consider the list and the catalog that Paul gives to describe the works of the flesh.

Sexual immorality (v. 19). The Greek word Paul uses here is *porneia*, which is a general term that refers to a broad category of sexual impurity. If I can simplify it, what he is referring to is adultery, fornication, dirty minds, dirty mouths. Paul also cites the related works of **impurity** and **sensuality** (v. 19).

Idolatry (v. 20) is whoredom against God. **Sorcery** (v. 20) is the use of magic. **Enmity** (v. 20), though it is not a physical thing, is a fleshly thing. Also on the list are **strife, jealousy, fits of anger** (v. 20). Are you subject, regularly, to **fits of anger**? Are you consumed in your heart by **jealousy**?

Rivalries, dissensions, divisions, envy (vv. 20–21). Doesn't it seem strange that God included in the ten most basic commandments to all humanity the command against coveting? We live in a world consumed by the politics of **envy**. We envy another person's job, another person's wealth, another person's house, another person's car, another person's bride or husband. That's of the flesh; that's our corruption coming out.

Drunkenness (v. 21). In Roman Catholic moral theology, drinking alcohol is not a sin, being tipsy is a venial sin, and being drunk is a mortal sin. I don't know where the line is between being tipsy and being drunk, but we better know the difference because **drunkenness** is of the flesh and is a sin.

Orgies (v. 21) were out-of-control festivals of debauchery often associated with the worship of pagan deities. They are not fitting for those who worship the one true God. And lest we think that this list of works of the flesh is exhaustive, Paul includes **things like these** (v. 21).

I warn you, as I warned you before, that those who do such things will not inherit the kingdom of God (v. 21). Paul, speaking with the authority of Jesus Christ, issues a stern warning that practitioners of these sinful works **will not inherit the kingdom of God**. That's how high the stakes are when we trifle with the works of the flesh.

Recently a local minister was in a discussion with two men who were "married" to each other. One said to the minister, "I'm going to go heaven, aren't I?" The minister said, "The cross covers everything." No, it doesn't. The cross covers the sins of the repentant, those who show by their lives that they belong to Christ. If you live a lifestyle of constant, impenitent, gross, and major sin, you will not get into the kingdom of God, because you have shown that you do not belong to Christ.

Paul is not saying here that if you've ever been envious, if you've ever been involved in fornication, if you've ever committed adultery, there's no hope for you. He's not saying that these are unforgivable sins. We know that these sins are forgivable. The sins that he lists here are forgivable, but they must be repented of. They're not just automatically forgiven. If your life is characterized and defined by these sins, you're in the flesh. If you stay in the flesh, you will never see the kingdom of God, let alone enter it.

19

THE FRUIT
OF THE SPIRIT

Galatians 5:22–26

~~~~~~

But the fruit of the Spirit is love, joy, peace, patience, kindness, goodness, faithfulness, gentleness, self-control; against such things there is no law. And those who belong to Christ Jesus have crucified the flesh with its passions and desires.

If we live by the Spirit, let us also keep in step with the Spirit. Let us not become conceited, provoking one another, envying one another.

When the Apostle Paul warned against living in the flesh, he delineated a list of the works of the flesh (Gal. 5:19–21). These were *works* that were plural. He was not saying that every person who lives in the flesh is a serial adulterer or a chronic drunkard. He mentioned different specific sins in which somebody can be caught up and ways of living that are unfitting for a lover of Christ.

In like manner, when the Bible speaks about the gifts of the Holy Spirit, the term *gifts* is in the plural because there's more than one gift that the Spirit bestows on individuals in the body of Christ (see Rom. 12:3–8; 1 Cor. 12; 1 Peter 4:10–11). Not every person who is a Christian receives every gift that the Holy Spirit has to offer or that the Spirit empowers. In the last century, we saw a tremendous increase in interest in the gifts of the Holy Spirit, and there was such interest that people were deeply persuaded to pursue particular gifts.

It's a good thing to want to know what gifts we have received from the Holy Spirit and to exercise whatever gifts we have. And yet, we seem to have had much more emphasis on the gifts of the Spirit, which can seem somewhat glamorous, than we have had on the fruit of the Spirit.

The fruit of the Spirit (v. 22) is mentioned in the singular, not the plural. That's an important distinction for us to notice. It's not as if one Christian is given the fruit of **love** and another one the fruit of **peace** and another one the fruit of **joy**. No, **the fruit of the Spirit** is a combined package. All the fruit of the Spirit is to be made manifest in the life of the Christian. There is, however, a way that believers do have multiple fruits—as evidence of their faith. A person may have just one gift, but they will display multiple fruits. These fruits are so important that Jesus Himself told us how we are to identify those who are in Christ and those who are merely giving lip service and making an empty profession of faith: "You will recognize them by their fruits" (Matt. 7:16).

The fruit of the Spirit is the result of the work of the Holy Spirit. Certainly, it is the Holy Spirit who causes us to be reborn. As Jesus told Nicodemus, "Unless one is born again he cannot see the kingdom of God" (John 3:3). We know that we are completely dependent upon the Holy Spirit's power of regeneration for our conversion, but that's not the end of the work of the Spirit.

Not only are we converted by the Holy Spirit, but we are indwelt by the Holy Spirit and empowered by the Holy Spirit; we are also being sanctified, made holy, made in conformity to Christ by the power of the Spirit. When Paul speaks about this, in this context, he's not just talking about virtues in general; nor is he talking about human achievements. Rather, he's talking about something that occurs supernaturally.

It is the power of the transcendent God who yields the fruit of the Spirit that Paul sets forth here. Several of these specific fruits are mentioned in the text. I think the first three are there for a reason, as they indicate the hierarchical aspect of the fruit of the Spirit. There's a sense in which the first three—**love, joy, peace**—are the foundation for the rest of the fruit of the Spirit being delineated by the Apostle.

The fruit of the Spirit is love (v. 22). Let me pause there. Does this mean that the only way anybody can ever have love is through the power of the Holy Spirit? All of us are commanded to love our neighbors as ourselves. This command is issued to the unregenerate person as well as the regenerate person. Even in our unregenerate state, we have abilities and capacities for affection that we might describe as love.

When I became a Christian, I was a freshman in college. Something happened to me. Along with the extraordinary reality of my own conversion, I found I had a whole new set of friends. I was engaged in a Bible study that met once a week at the local church to study the Scriptures. We sang hymns and we prayed for an extensive period of time. A certain bond developed among those of us who were involved in this prayer group.

I remember how radically different my life was from what it had been in high school. When I was in high school, if you weren't an athlete, I wasn't interested in you because, in my opinion, you weren't worth very much. I defined human value in terms of sports. Soon after my conversion, I realized that my closest and dearest friends were not the athletes on campus anymore but were the Christians.

When my wife came to Christ, she had the same experience. All of a sudden, she had deep bonds with friends who were unlike the normal group with whom she had previously associated. Guys who played together on athletic teams have a certain camaraderie, as do people who served together in the armed forces or in police corps.

But when Paul talks about the fruit of the Spirit, he's talking about an extra dimension, a transcendent capacity for love that is different. Calvin talked about unconverted people displaying what he called civic or civil righteousness. People don't have to be Christians to make sacrifices for the benefit of their neighbors, but again there is a distinction between civic or civil virtue and the virtue that comes through the power of the Holy Ghost who is forming us and shaping us for our ultimate destiny of glorification.

The love of which the Apostle is speaking here is at a different dimension. It's a love that has concern, regard, compassion, and, as we see later in the passage, loyalty to the body of Christ that we call the communion of saints. If you're a Christian, Christ is in you and you are in Christ. If I'm a Christian, Christ is in me and I am in Christ. How can I possibly hate somebody who is in Christ and Christ is in that person? Our very bond as Christians in the communion of saints makes it next to impossible to espouse hatred in our hearts for someone who is also part of the beloved in Christ.

At the front of the list is the fruit of **love**. Paul devotes an entire chapter, 1 Corinthians 13, to explain what it means to have this love. I confess that, in one sense, 1 Corinthians 13 is one of my least favorite passages in all of sacred Scripture. I hear it extolled and recited at weddings, and many people say it's their favorite chapter. But when I read that passage, I'm wounded by almost every stroke of the Apostle's pen. Love does not seek its own benefit. Love is patient, tender, and kind. These are all things that I would like to be, but just as the law reveals our sin, so the perfect expression of love that we find in 1 Corinthians 13 shows how high this standard of love really is.

Our culture tends to define love as a noun. It's something that we feel. It's a feeling that we have. It's something we fall into. We describe love as a feeling, but in the Scriptures, the concept of love is better understood as a verb than a noun. It's how we act. It's what we do with respect to our brothers and sisters.

Then Paul goes on to speak of **joy** (v. 22). For some of us the word is almost a foreign term, but there's no excuse to ever be a dour Christian. Joy is foundational to the Christian life. Joy is something that is basic, so all-consuming in the Christian life that it is also a transcendent reality, something that transcends all the temporary difficulties that we experience as we go through the travails of this world.

The Bible says Jesus was "a man of sorrows and acquainted with grief" (Isa. 53:3). When we read that, we may think that if that's the case, then Jesus Himself possibly didn't possess joy, the fruit of the Holy Spirit. But even in Jesus' darkest hour, the joy of His soul was never, ever extinguished. There is an inner delight that every Christian understands and feels for God, and even Job cried out, "Though he slay me, I will hope in him" (Job 13:15).

That's what comes of having a supernatural element of joy. Joy doesn't just describe a person who exhibits happiness all the time. Happiness is a fleeting, earthly emotion, whereas joy is related to blessedness, the supreme, transcendent gift of favor and settledness from God. For the Christian, blessedness captures the supernatural fruit of the Holy Spirit that is joy.

If you are a Christian, you have that fruit, though it may be exhibited in various ways and to various degrees over the course of your life. Even in the darkest night of the soul, the joy that God the Holy Spirit creates in the soul of the Christian can never be eradicated. Christians are a joyous people.

Third, Paul talks of **peace** (v. 22). The Bible speaks about various kinds of peace. There's what Luther spoke of: a carnal or fleshly peace. It is like the peace of the Old Testament false prophets who gave the people of Israel the message they wanted to hear. The false prophets said, "Peace, peace," when there was no peace (Jer. 6:14).

When the Bible speaks about peace in the supernatural sense, it speaks about a peace that is beyond comprehension, a peace that passes understanding. This was the last will and testament of Jesus our Lord, our legacy, when He died. In John 14, Jesus said to His disciples: "Let not your hearts be troubled. Believe in God; believe also in me" (v. 1), and He talked about His Father's house having many mansions; then He said, "Peace I leave with you; my peace I give to you" (v. 27). He didn't just say "peace" but "*my* peace I give to you." No wonder He is called the Prince of Peace, because nobody ever communicated the depths and the riches of the peace of God more than Jesus did. He could even tame the storm by simply opening His mouth and saying: "Peace! Be still!" (Mark 4:39).

When we look at Paul's teaching on the doctrine of justification in Romans 5, he expresses the very first fruit of our justification: "Since we have been justified by faith, we have peace with God through our Lord Jesus Christ" (v. 1). The war's over. It's not a temporal peace that will vanish the first time somebody rattles a sword. When God makes peace with the believer, it lasts forever.

That's a fruit that we have. It's not just inner peace or peace from inner turmoil but, ultimately, peace with God. I can grieve the Holy Spirit or disappoint the Father, but once we are reconciled through the blood of Christ, God never picks up His sword again, and His wrath is no more. Reconciliation has been provided for us in Christ, but it takes our unconditional surrender to the Father and to the Son, that we may gain the fruit of peace with God.

Patience (v. 22). The more correct word in the Greek is not just patience but "long-suffering." Long-suffering presupposes that we're under attack. That attack might seem to be endless and without respite, but the Holy Spirit makes it possible for us to be patient in ways that the flesh doesn't; the Spirit enables us to imitate the very long-suffering that God has with us with each other.

Kindness (v. 22). I love that word. I want to be a kind person. I don't want to be known for being mean. I hope it will be chiseled on my tombstone: "This was a kind man." But if there's any kindness in me, it's only because of the Spirit of God, who melts our wrath, calms our spirits, and makes it possible for us to be kind and its corollary, to be gentle.

Goodness, faithfulness, gentleness (vv. 22–23). Here the word **faithfulness** basically means loyalty. In the Old Testament, one of the richest words in the Hebrew language is *hesed*. It refers to God's loving-kindness, or His covenant loyalty. Another translation is "steadfast love." Listen to the psalmist cry out: "Have mercy on me, O God, according to your steadfast love" (Ps. 51:1). He's asking for *hesed*. He's asking for that loyal commitment that God has made to His people. It's a commitment that no matter how much I am inclined to betray God, He has never betrayed me. I can point to people who have betrayed me, whom I have betrayed, but never once can I accuse God of the sin of betrayal. He's loyal, and when He loves us, He loves us to the end.

Self-control; against such things there is no law (v. 23). There's no rule against being kind. God doesn't command that we never be gentle. There's no law against tender mercy and long-suffering. We never have to fear the consequences of the law of God when we walk not in the flesh but in the Spirit, bringing forth the Spirit's fruit in its season.

And those who belong to Christ Jesus have crucified the flesh (v. 24). The flesh is not annihilated. We know that, but it's under a death sentence. The passions of the flesh have been nailed to the cross, and we are crucified with Christ in our flesh.

If we live by the Spirit, let us also keep in step with the Spirit (v. 25). It's important for soldiers to march in step, but what is really important is for us to **keep in step with the Spirit**. If we want to walk with the Spirit, we don't want to be sloppy about it. We are called by Paul to keep in step.

Let us not become conceited, provoking one another, envying one another (v. 26). In brief terms, this is the fruit of the Spirit, and it should be our goal to grow in that fruit every day of our lives.

20

THE HOUSEHOLD
OF FAITH

Galatians 6:1–5

Brothers, if anyone is caught in any transgression, you who are spiritual should restore him in a spirit of gentleness. Keep watch on yourself, lest you too be tempted. Bear one another's burdens, and so fulfill the law of Christ. For if anyone thinks he is something, when he is nothing, he deceives himself. But let each one test his own work, and then his reason to boast will be in himself alone and not in his neighbor. For each will have to bear his own load.

The sixteenth century saw the greatest split in the history of the church with the Protestant Reformation. What resulted from the Reformation was not two ecclesiastical communities but several. There was the church in Germany, the church in Scotland, the church in England, the church in Switzerland, and so on. A question arose at that time since there were so many different churches: What is it that constitutes a valid church? Stated differently: What are the necessary ingredients for a church to be a church?

Among the Protestant Reformers, there were differences of opinion regarding church polity, understandings of the law, and various points of theology. The Reformers concluded that the bare minimum that defines a valid or a true church is the following things: number one, that the gospel is truly preached; number two, that the sacraments are duly administered; and number three, that church discipline be exercised. The Reformers agreed that if the church did not administer discipline according to the Word of God, it didn't qualify to be a valid church.

In the sixteenth century, church discipline was severe. I visited a museum of torture in Rothenburg ob der Tauber, Germany. It included different devices that were used to inflict pain, principally to discipline people in the church. The Spanish Inquisition had no hesitation in using these kinds of devices. The final act of discipline was burning at the stake. Even though we look back on that period and think that the disciplinary measures were extraordinarily severe, nevertheless, to understand it, you have to understand that the church in the sixteenth century believed in a real hell. They believed that it was justifiable to use any kind of discipline of the body to save the soul. In other words, these devices of torture were administered to try to lead sinners to repentance, that their souls might be saved.

Today, we don't see much of that thing in the church. The tendency seems to be when periods of discipline are severe, the next generation will be lax in discipline. If this generation is lax, then the next generation will gravitate toward severity. It was Christ Himself who instituted principles and guidelines for discipline in the church. Yet at the same time, He warned that the visible church will always contain wheat and chaff. There will be goats along with the sheep. Augustine said that the church is a *corpus permixtum*, a mixed body that will always contain unbelievers who make professions of faith. That's why he distinguished between the visible church and the invisible church. The invisible church consists of all true believers in all times and places. It is invisible to us, but it's not invisible to God. We can't read the hearts of our fellow members. The visible church, by contrast, consists of all professing believers, together with their children. The visible church is the province of church discipline.

Jesus warned that though discipline should take place in the church, it ought to be done with the greatest care for fear that the sheep (true believers, members of the invisible church) would be confused with the goats (unbelievers, some of whom are members of the visible church) and the wheat would be chastened along with the chaff. In Matthew 18, Jesus speaks about some of the basic principles of discipline:

> "If your brother sins against you, go and tell him his fault, between you
> and him alone. If he listens to you, you have gained your brother. But
> if he does not listen, take one or two others along with you, that every
> charge may be established by the evidence of two or three witnesses. If he
> refuses to listen to them, tell it to the church. And if he refuses to listen

even to the church, let him be to you as a Gentile and a tax collector. Truly, I say to you, whatever you bind on earth shall be bound in heaven, and whatever you loose on earth shall be loosed in heaven. Again I say to you, if two of you agree on earth about anything they ask, it will be done for them by my Father in heaven." (vv. 15–19)

Jesus continues in verse 20, "For where two or three are gathered in my name, there am I among them." This verse is often used to indicate that if two or three Christians get together for a prayer meeting or some other religious assembly, we can be sure that the Lord is present. That's a legitimate application, but we often forget the context, which had to do with exercising church discipline. The most difficult part of the business of the church is to exercise church discipline. It ought not to be done in a precipitous way, so that's when we need to appeal to Jesus for His presence and for His help.

As seen in these passages, church discipline has certain steps that are taken in order. We are not to rush to judgment. We don't immediately cut an offender off from the body of Christ. There is a process, which is always to be driven by a desire to restore a person to the fullness of faith and involvement in the church community.

Paul deals with the question of church discipline in 1 Corinthians. A problem had arisen in the church in Corinth: "It is actually reported that there is sexual immorality among you, and of a kind that is not tolerated even among pagans, for a man has his father's wife. And you are arrogant! Ought you not rather to mourn? Let him who has done this be removed from among you" (5:1–2). News came to the Apostle Paul that there was incest going on in the Corinthian church. Not only was it going on and openly manifest, but it was tolerated by the church. The Apostle had to write to the Corinthians and direct the church to put the offender outside the fellowship of the church—that is, to excommunicate him.

If the pendulum is swinging toward any direction in our day, it's in the direction of laxity. Not too long ago, I talked to a friend who was a member of another local church. He had a girlfriend and was living with her outside the bonds of marriage. I asked my friend, "Does your pastor know that you're living with this woman who's not your wife?" He smiled and said: "Well, sure he does. We don't do judgment in my church." That is to say, we don't discipline people who are living in open, scandalous immorality. That's usually the rule of the day.

After hearing the stinging rebuke of the Apostle Paul, the Corinthian community excommunicated the sinner. But the goal of discipline is always restoration. We want to lead people to repentance. We want to encourage them to return and be a part of the body of Christ when they repent. Paul ordered the discipline of the man in Corinth, and the church excommunicated him. He repented, which is exactly the goal. But the Corinthians wouldn't receive him back in the church. They fell off one side of the horse, and when they got on again, they fell off the other side of the horse. Paul had to write in 2 Corinthians: "This person has repented. He's been forgiven. Receive him back in the church" (see 2:5–11). We have to learn about these matters, and we must be jealous and zealous at all times to seek the restoration of those who have been tempted.

Brothers, if anyone is caught in any transgression (v. 1). Peter taught that "love covers a multitude of sins" (1 Peter 4:8). You don't go to the church and begin the process of discipline over every peccadillo. Jesus makes it clear that there are greater and lesser sins (see Matt. 23:23–26). If the goal is to prosecute every transgression that occurs in the church, the church would have no time to do anything except church discipline. Even when discipline is begun, it's only begun for serious matters. Although every sin is serious in one sense, we're not supposed to be threatening discipline for trivial matters.

The attitude we are to have is "there but for the grace of God go I." The only way that any of us can stand in the presence of God is by His grace, and thus we are called to exhibit patience and humility and goodness.

It is sometimes said that the Christian church is the only army that shoots its own wounded. A pastor asked me at the beginning of my ministry: "What do you think the church is? Do you think the church is an army or do you think it's a hospital?" I said: "Yes. If the church triumphant is ever going to be the church triumphant, it has to first be the church militant. We are an army. We are in warfare. We are fighting against powers and principalities and spiritual wickedness in high places, but the church also has to be a hospital. We are not to shoot our own wounded."

You who are spiritual should restore him in a spirit of gentleness (v. 1). This call for restoration presupposes that the person who has been disciplined repents and comes back to the body of Christ. There is really only one sin for which a person is ever excommunicated from the fellowship of the body of Christ, and that is contumacy. Contumacy is being persistently impenitent. Every church has a governing body, and in my church the governing body is the session. If the session goes through every step of discipline but there is no repentance and the sinner is persistently impenitent, then and only then does the final stage of excommunication take place. Even that is with the hope that the act of excommunication will lead the person to repent of the sin for which he or she was disciplined in the first place. Then the person can be restored to the body of Christ.

When we celebrate the Lord's Supper, one of the things that pastors are always to do is called "fencing the table." It is the duty of a pastor when administering the sacrament of the Lord's Supper to warn the congregation that the Lord's Supper is a special sacrament given by Christ to His church. We are warned by Paul in 1 Corinthians that if we don't discern the Lord's body, if we eat and drink in unbelief, we are eating and drinking unto damnation (11:27–29). The Lord's Supper is a discernment sacrament. We are not simply to go through the motions of a particular liturgy. This is holy ground. If you're not a believer and you participate in the Lord's Supper, you're mocking God. That's a blasphemous thing to do.

That doesn't mean that you have to be sinless to come to the Lord's Table. We are to examine ourselves to see that our profession of faith is genuine, and in humility we come to the Lord's Table to have a fresh sense of our forgiveness of sins, of the remission of our sin. Fencing the table involves asking unbelievers and those who are under the discipline of another evangelical church not to partake of the Lord's Supper. This is part of the process of church discipline. One of the steps of church discipline is that an offender is, for a season, suspended from the Lord's Supper until he repents.

I know that if a person is suspended from the Lord's Supper at one church, he can find other churches that will serve the sacrament to him and won't honor the discipline of this particular church. We must try to be careful in honoring the discipline of every church that we're involved with. If someone is from another church and he is under the discipline of that church and that comes to our attention, we want to make sure that we honor the ministry that is going on in the other church.

Often the attitude is this: What I do in my private life is none of the church's business. However, the business of the church is the spiritual well-being and the spiritual care of the flock. It is the responsibility of the church elders to protect and watch over the sheep.

21

MOCKING GOD

Galatians 6:6–10

Let the one who is taught the word share all good things with the one who teaches. Do not be deceived: God is not mocked, for whatever one sows, that will he also reap. For the one who sows to his own flesh will from the flesh reap corruption, but the one who sows to the Spirit will from the Spirit reap eternal life. And let us not grow weary of doing good, for in due season we will reap, if we do not give up. So then, as we have opportunity, let us do good to everyone, and especially to those who are of the household of faith.

Let the one who is taught the word share all good things with the one who teaches (v. 6). Having called his readers to walk in the Spirit and not in the flesh, Paul in verse 6 makes a statement that hangs there like a dangling participle. It's not clear exactly how it fits with what went before it and what comes after it.

In this verse, Paul makes mention of those who are ministering to the church, those who are the *didaskoloi*, the teachers of the people of God. Paul lays down the basic foundation for the financial support of the ministry of the gospel. He is concerned because, already in the first century, there was a problem with those who were benefiting from the Word of God being reluctant to render support for those who were teaching them the Word of God. This has been true in the church for all ages.

The latest statistic I saw was that the two groups of professional people in the United States who were the least compensated for their labor were first ministers and second teachers. In the Old Testament, we see that God instituted a tithe, and the tithe was to support the priests and the teachers because, in the Old Testament, the church and the state were one, and education and ministry in the temple were all supported by the tithe.

I've often wondered why God did that instead of leaving the principle of supporting the teachers and the preachers or ministers to the free market. My conclusion is that people, not just in America, but throughout the world, do not attach a high value to the services performed by ministers and by teachers.

Calvin talked about concerns of his day when preachers and teachers were struggling, and he raised this question: "How do we understand this poverty of value that those who treat the souls, who impart eternal benefits, are neglected, but those who treat the body are well supported?" It was true in the sixteenth century, in the seventeenth century, and in the first century, and it's true today.

Do not be deceived: God is not mocked, for whatever one sows, that will he also reap (v. 7). Luther said that there was no problem for people who were serving Satan, those who were false teachers in the church who prospered greatly, but if the preacher was faithful to the truth of the gospel, he could expect to live a penurious existence. This is such a serious matter that some commentators say that what Paul is saying is that verse 7 is specifically addressing verse 6 and the issue of those who do not support the work of the ministry. That very well may be, but I don't agree. I think verse 7 goes back to the end of chapter 5, where he's talking about the cumulative problem with the flesh and the Spirit, that there are many works of the flesh that should draw us to great diligence and vigilance.

Do not be deceived. This is not the first time the Apostle has expressed concern for deception in this epistle to the Galatians. Earlier he said: "Oh foolish Galatians! Who has bewitched you?" (3:1). Here again, he's talking about being bewitched in the sense of being severely and radically deceived. The greatest deceiver of all is Satan, the father of lies. He is the master of deception. The greatest lie is that the gospel doesn't matter—we can live without it, we don't need Christ, we don't need the things of God, and what there is now is all there will ever be.

People are deceived all the time, and Paul warns us against this deception. The biggest thing he's concerned about with respect to deception is this: **God is not mocked**. Paul is not saying that nobody ever mocks God. That is contrary to the evidence. The whole world is engaged in the business of mocking God every day, of slandering the eternal holiness and goodness and blessedness of God. We use His name for a curse word. We walk through this world having very little respect for the character and the nature of God.

When Paul says God is not mocked, he is saying that God won't put up with being mocked. You may mock God. You may be irreverent and not take Him or His Word seriously, and you may think that you can get away with it. God, however, will not tolerate such mocking.

Psalm 2 asks, "Why do the nations rage and the peoples plot in vain? The kings of the earth set themselves, and the rulers take counsel together" (vv. 1–2). The kings of the earth "set themselves." The language describes cosmic rebellion. This is how the psalmist describes the rulers of this earth who plot together in vain.

"Vain" can be used in two different ways. There is this boldness of vanity that comes from pride, but there's also the use of the term "vain" that is a synonym for "futile." The world leaders come together for such a futile purpose, but what is this international conspiracy of which the psalmist writes in Psalm 2? "The kings of the earth set themselves, and the rulers take counsel together, against the Lord and against his Anointed" (v. 2). Satan is the prince of the power of the air. He's the god of this world, and he has the rulers and the leaders of this world in his service. They gather together and assert themselves defiantly against God and against His Anointed—that is, against God and against His Christ. I wonder how many days we have left in this country where we'll be able to freely preach the gospel. So much hostility is being raised in our own country against God and against Christ.

Psalm 2 continues, "Let us burst their bonds apart and cast away their cords from us" (v. 3). That is figurative language referring to a declaration of independence from God. We are apart from God, not under God. We are anti-God, and we've had our hands tied by religion, by Christianity, by the Word of God. Let's burst those ropes and cast those cords away from us. That's the statement of those who have their hearts set against Christ and against His Word. It's a universal mocking of God. This is not the time for us to say, "Look at what those bad people do." We were, by nature, estranged from God. It was our nature in the flesh to say that we wanted to cast God out of our thinking. We didn't want Him intruding into our lives. We didn't want Him ruling our behavior. We wanted to be free.

How does God respond to that? God looks down from heaven and sees the collective missiles and bombs and artillery aimed at heaven. The nations come together thinking they're going to get rid of God. Psalm 2 says, "He who sits in the heavens laughs; the Lord holds them in derision" (v. 4). It's as though the God of heaven and earth looks down at the conglomeration of weapons aimed in His direction, and He takes His finger and wipes them out as though they were only so many insects and says, "Do you think that you have the power to overthrow My eternal, omnipotent reign?" The Lord God omnipotent reigns whether we like it or don't like it, whether we revolt against it or acquiesce to it.

This is a tragic comedy that ends with the laughter of God. "Then he will speak to them in his wrath, and terrify them in his fury, saying, 'As for me, I have set my King on Zion, my holy hill'" (vv. 5–6). Jesus is God's King. God the Father has established Jesus as the King of His kingdom, and no one in heaven or earth has the power to take that kingdom away.

Do not be deceived: God is not mocked. He's not going to put up with this. Paul goes on to borrow a metaphor from the agrarian culture in which he lived and says, **For whatever one sows, that will he also reap** (v. 7).

One of the most brilliant people I've met is Stephen Meyer, writer of two extremely important books, *Signature in the Cell* and *Darwin's Doubt*. He is one of the dominant voices in the defense of the concept of intelligent design.

Two of the leading twentieth-century atheists from Britain, Antony Flew and A.J. Ayer, both came to theism in their later years, both on the basis that they couldn't deny the teleological manifestation of design in the universe. Ayer and his comrade said that without intelligent design, nature is unintelligible. That is to say, you can't have science if there's no real intelligent design in the universe.

Where does Meyer get this proof for intelligent design? If you carefully read his books (they're complicated and difficult), they give an almost exhaustive examination of DNA. DNA involves actual information that is found at the cellular level. The things in this world, particularly in the world of biology and zoology, do not just happen by natural selection; they happen by information, by a designated code within the cell that causes things to be what they are.

The philosopher Aristotle's most famous pupil was Alexander the Great. When Alexander went on his Hellenization program to convert the whole world to Greek thinking and to the Greek language, he included an army of scientists on this world mission at the behest of Aristotle. Wherever Alexander went, he took scientists with him to collect flora and fauna, which he took back to Aristotle so that Aristotle and his teachers could analyze the specimens.

What Aristotle came up with more than two thousand years before Stephen Meyer was this question: Why, if you plant an acorn in the ground, doesn't it produce an elephant? Have you ever wondered about that? Why do I expect to see an oak tree if I plant an acorn? Aristotle theorized that every seed contains a tiny element of intelligence. That's why if you plant orange seeds, you're not going to get a grapevine; rather, as expected, you get oranges.

Paul is pointing to this clear truth when he says, **Whatever one sows, that will he also reap.** This is the biggest deception that we all face. We think that we can sow one thing and get something else. Paul said there's a corollary, unmistakable and immutable, between what you sow and what you reap. He compares this to the flesh and the Spirit by saying, **For the one who sows to his own flesh will from the flesh reap corruption, but the one who sows to the Spirit will from the Spirit reap eternal life. And let us not grow weary of doing good, for in due season we will reap, if we do not give up** (vv. 8–9).

I have a monthly column in *Tabletalk* magazine called Right Now Counts Forever. The modern existentialist mantra is that right now counts for right now, which means it counts for nothing. But we are creatures made for eternity. Jesus Himself told us to lay up for ourselves treasures in heaven. The people that Paul is addressing weren't going to support the preaching of the gospel. They wanted to hold on to their earthly goods, to squeeze them as tightly as they could, and they didn't think about investing in heaven.

Everything in this world perishes. Only that which is true lives forever, and so what we do today, what we sow today, matters forever. Don't be deceived. Don't be fooled. What we sow, we will surely reap.

22

BIG LETTERS

Galatians 6:11–18

See with what large letters I am writing to you with my own hand. It is those who want to make a good showing in the flesh who would force you to be circumcised, and only in order that they may not be persecuted for the cross of Christ. For even those who are circumcised do not themselves keep the law, but they desire to have you circumcised that they may boast in your flesh. But far be it from me to boast except in the cross of our Lord Jesus Christ, by which the world has been crucified to me, and I to the world. For neither circumcision counts for anything, nor uncircumcision, but a new creation. And as for all who walk by this rule, peace and mercy be upon them, and upon the Israel of God.

From now on let no one cause me trouble, for I bear on my body the marks of Jesus. The grace of our Lord Jesus Christ be with your spirit, brothers. Amen.

When Paul picked up his stylus to write this letter meant for circulation throughout the region of Galatia, I can't imagine it ever came into his mind that, two thousand years later, we would be studying this epistle word for word, line upon line, paragraph upon paragraph, seeking to understand what was disclosed through him and by him. But here we are, all these centuries later, still feasting on the Word of God as it is found in the book of Galatians.

Martin Luther wrote scores of books in his lifetime, and two times he wrote a complete commentary on the book of Galatians, one in 1519 and another in 1535; he called the second volume of Galatians his Katie von Bora. Luther named the volume after his wife because it was his favorite of those books he authored. When we study Galatians and understand the central significance of the gospel that was at stake at this time, we understand why Luther called it his Katie von Bora.

See with what large letters I am writing to you with my own hand (v. 11). Paul speaks of the large letters that he uses to write, presumably not simply for the closing testimony but for the entire epistle. He's calling attention to his handwriting. What's the significance of that?

Scholars have puzzled over this for centuries. There are different theories. One is that Paul, with all his infirmities and all that he suffered through the beatings and the whippings and the stonings he had endured, was perhaps left in a state of near blindness and had to write large letters so that he could read them himself. Others think that his fingers were injured by all the tortures he experienced and that he perhaps found difficulty in writing. We also know that it was customary for the Apostle not to write his own letters but to dictate them to an amanuensis, or secretary, and then he would sign his name at the end. However, in this case he calls particular attention to the use of large letters in his writing.

Another theory is that large letters indicated emphasis. We've seen that this was the most emphatic epistle that the Apostle wrote. It was the one about which he was most exercised and most grieved. The Judaizers were doing everything they could not only to undermine Paul's authority but to undermine the gospel. This is what moved the Apostle to such great urgency: he was fighting for the gospel itself.

It is those who want to make a good showing in the flesh who would force you to be circumcised, and only in order that they may not be persecuted for the cross of Christ (v. 12). Earlier in the epistle, in the first chapter, Paul wrote:

> I am astonished that you are so quickly deserting him who called you in the grace of Christ and are turning to a different gospel—not that there is another one, but there are some who trouble you and want to distort the gospel of Christ. But even if we or an angel from heaven should preach to you a gospel contrary to the one we preached to you, let him be accursed. As we have said before, so now I say again: If anyone is preaching to you a gospel contrary to the one you received, let him be accursed.
>
> For am I now seeking the approval of man, or of God? Or am I trying to please man? If I were still trying to please man, I would not be a servant of Christ. (vv. 6–10)

He starts the epistle with extremely strong language. Remember, he emphatically raised the question in the first chapter about who the Galatian heretics were trying to please. The answer was clear. They had no desire to please God. The one concern that drove their spirits was to please men.

Paul says of the Judaizers, "You people who are teaching this distorted view of the gospel are doing it because the gospel is offensive to those who hear it, and you don't want to give any offense; you want to please everybody around you, and that is a work of the flesh not of the Spirit." He goes on to say that they want to make a good showing in the flesh so that they may not be persecuted for the cross of Christ. We know something of the first-century history of the Christian church, of the martyrdoms that were suffered by believers under the tyranny of the Roman government. Nero used Christians as human torches to illumine his gardens at night, and the Colosseum was used for the entertainment of the emperor and Roman citizens who enjoyed watching Christians being devoured by lions or killed by gladiators.

All that is standard history, but we often overlook that in the first years of the expansion of the Christian church, it wasn't the Romans who were involved in persecuting Christians; it was initially the Jewish authorities. One of the reasons the Jewish authorities were persecuting Christians is that, from the outside, it appeared that Christianity was simply a sect of Judaism. The Jews wanted to repudiate that belief. When Paul, after his conversion, went from place to place and city to city, he was initially persecuted by the Jewish authorities. He was beaten with rods and stoned, and those in Galatia understood that if you identified with the gospel that Paul preached and with Christ and with the idea of justification by faith alone and not through the works of the law, you were risking physical torment and possibly death.

Paul says: "I know what these people are up to. They want you to follow the ceremonial laws so that there won't be trouble with the Jewish authorities and they will escape the persecution that I have endured for years, the persecution that our Lord Himself endured." The compromise was this: embrace the Jewish ceremonial law and you may not be persecuted for the cross of Christ. That was the scandal: the cross. That was the shame that every Christian endured if he stood in the shadow of the cross and associated with the scandal of the cross; he could expect to suffer the humiliation of the cross.

For even those who are circumcised do not themselves keep the law, but they desire to have you circumcised that they may boast in your flesh (v. 13). The Judaizers were obviously disobedient to the moral law, yet they wanted to insist upon meticulous observation of the ceremonial law. They were not law-abiding at all. Further, they desired to **boast in** the Galatians' **flesh**. It is

as if they were saying: "Here are my converts, those Christians who were being
led away from the ceremonial law. I've persuaded them to submit to circumcision." They wanted to parade around their trophies of accomplishment in the
Jewish community, and Paul didn't like boasting. He wrote in 1 Corinthians
1:31, "Let the one who boasts, boast in the Lord." We don't have anything else
to boast about.

**But far be it from me to boast except in the cross of our Lord Jesus Christ,
by which the world has been crucified to me, and I to the world** (v. 14).
Though Paul did not want to be involved in boasting, he made one exception:
except in the cross of our Lord Jesus Christ. For the unbeliever, the cross
is equated with scandal. For Paul, it was the highest source of personal pride.
Christ and His cross were the only things worth boasting about for Paul.

By which the world has been crucified to me, and I to the world. This
is a strange saying. Paul says that not only was Christ crucified, but in a real
sense, *he* was crucified with Christ; in addition, not only was he crucified with
Christ, but *the whole world* was crucified with Christ, and, in the crucifixion,
the world died to Paul and Paul died to the world.

The Jews had a radical concept of corporate solidarity. They were not rugged
isolationists who saw themselves only as individuals. In the Old Testament,
there was this idea of the fellowship of believers in the household of God;
there was unity. When Paul speaks throughout his epistles, he talks about the
union that we have with Christ. If you're a Christian, Christ is in you and
you are in Christ. What does that mean? Somehow, I as a Christian am truly
related—transcendentally, spiritually—to another human being who lived two
thousand years ago. I am in Christ and He is in me. We're not saying that Jesus
lives in my heart or in my memory. There is a transcendental, spiritual reality
that God speaks about, and it is this: Jesus Christ dwells in my heart, and I am
not just related to Jesus by covenant, but there is a real spiritual union between
Christ and me.

That's why we have the doctrine of the communion of saints because, if I'm
in Christ and you're in Christ, and Christ is in me and Christ is in you, then
what does that say about our relationship? We have a solidarity, a special spiritual
communion, that transcends the flesh and transcends the world. When Jesus
was crucified that day outside the city gates of Jerusalem, we were crucified
with Him because God took our real guilt and our real sins and put it upon
our Savior so that in His death, we died. That's what Paul talks about when he
says, "I have been crucified with Christ" (2:20). We also have been crucified
with Christ. Then Paul goes on further to say that not only is the day that
Jesus died the day he died, but it's the day the world died in him and in every

believer. As Paul expounded in Galatians 5 on the works of the flesh and the fruit of the Spirit, he made a sharp distinction between the kingdom of God and the city of man. Paul is now saying that the world, the flesh, the devil have been put to death for the Christian.

"The world doesn't live for me anymore," Paul is saying, "and I don't live for this world." We talk about being in the world but not of the world, and yet we also use terms like *worldly*. If you're a worldly person, you need to examine your soul because, if you're worldly, that means you're still in love with the world and with the flesh and you haven't allowed the world to be crucified with you.

For neither circumcision counts for anything, nor uncircumcision, but a new creation (v. 15). That's what he has been saying throughout this entire epistle. The Galatian Judaizers wanted to make everything hinge on circumcision, and Paul tells them that they missed the whole point of the gospel. You're not saved by circumcision; you're not saved by not being circumcised. In the final judgment, it's not going to matter whether you're circumcised or uncircumcised.

What matters is this: Are you **a new creation**? September 13, 1957, I was born a second time. I read 2 Corinthians, and the text that jumped out at me was these words from Paul: "From now on, therefore, we regard no one according to the flesh. Even though we once regarded Christ according to the flesh, we regard him thus no longer. Therefore, if anyone is in Christ, he is a new creation. The old has passed away; behold, the new has come. All this is from God" (5:16–18).

The whole point of this epistle to the Galatians is to put the flesh to death and to walk in the Spirit. If you are a Christian, you can't be a Christian apart from the power of the Holy Ghost. Unless the Holy Spirit changes the disposition of your heart, you will never come to Christ. Nobody comes to Christ by simply making a decision, raising their hand, or walking an aisle. Rebirth is only by the power of God the Holy Spirit, who changes your nature from flesh to Spirit. As Jesus told Nicodemus, "That which is born of the flesh is flesh, and that which is born of the Spirit is spirit" (John 3:6). That's why Jesus told Nicodemus he had to be born again. Paul comes back to this concept right here in the conclusion of his epistle. **For neither circumcision counts for anything, nor uncircumcision, but a new creation**.

And as for all who walk by this rule, peace and mercy be upon them, and upon the Israel of God (v. 16). **The Israel of God** is not limited to the Jews who were circumcised. The Israel of God is the whole body of Christ, Jew and Gentile, all who are converted. All who are in Christ Jesus make up the new Israel, the new creation that God has brought to pass.

From now on let no one cause me trouble, for I bear on my body the marks of Jesus (v. 17). Paul says he's had enough trouble. He could open his shirt, take off his hat, and say: "Look at this gash; look at this scar. I walk with a limp, I speak with difficulty, and I see poorly. I'm like a walking dead man. I have many marks that I have suffered for your sake and for the sake of the gospel, so please stop it. Let's have no more."

Then, Paul ends with the tersest final benediction of all his epistles: **The grace of our Lord Jesus Christ be with your spirit, brothers. Amen** (v. 18).

INDEX OF NAMES

ABOUT THE AUTHOR

Dr. R.C. Sproul was founder of Ligonier Ministries, founding pastor of Saint Andrew's Chapel in Sanford, Fla., first president of Reformation Bible College, and executive editor of *Tabletalk* magazine. His radio program, *Renewing Your Mind*, is still broadcast daily on hundreds of radio stations around the world and can also be heard online. He was author of more than one hundred books, including *The Holiness of God*, *Chosen by God*, and *Everyone's a Theologian*. He was recognized throughout the world for his articulate defense of the inerrancy of Scripture and the need for God's people to stand with conviction upon His Word.